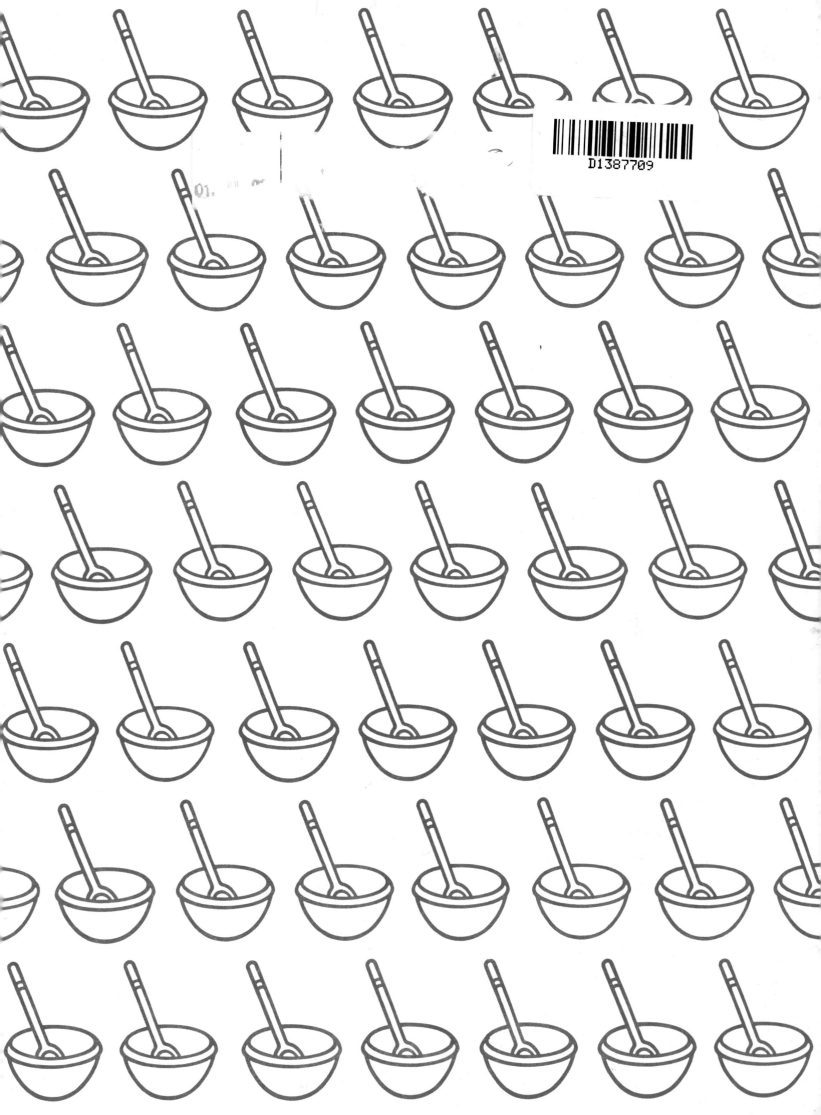

T H E
ESSENTIAL
MICROWAVE
HANDBOOK

THE
ESSENTIAL
MICROWAVE
HANDBOOK

THE COMPLETE GUIDE TO
MICROWAVE COOKING

Carol Bowen

HERMES
HOUSE

This edition published in 1998 by Hermes House

Hermes House is an imprint of
Anness Publishing Limited
Hermes House
88–89 Blackfriars Road
London SE1 8HA

A CIP catalogue record for this book is available from the British Library

ISBN 1 84038 122 1

Publisher: Joanna Lorenz
Senior Editor: Linda Fraser
Editor: Bridget Jones
Designer: William Mason
Illustrator: Madeleine David

Printed and bound in Singapore

3 5 7 9 10 8 6 4 2

NOTES
For all recipes, quantities are given in both metric and imperial measures and, where
appropriate, measures are also given in standard cups and spoons. Follow one set, but
not a mixture, because they are not interchangeable.

Standard spoon and cup measures are level.
1 tsp = 5ml, 1 tbsp = 15ml, 1 cup = 250ml/8fl oz

Australian standard tablespoons are 20ml. Australian readers should use 3 tsp in place
of 1 tbsp for measuring small quantities of gelatine, cornflour, salt, etc.

Size 3 (medium) eggs are used unless otherwise stated.

Contents

Introduction

Undeniably, speed is the main advantage of microwave cooking; however, it is not this in isolation that has made microwaves the success story they are. Not only do microwaves make light work of cooking many staple dishes and family favourites, but they also cook them to perfection. With a microwave cooker, limp, soggy greens, over-sticky rice, nutritionally poor fruit-based desserts and labour- and time-intensive meat, fish and poultry dishes are things of the past; these emerge from the microwave fresh, colourful, nutritionally rich and, moreover, most appetizing. The time-saving aspect may be great, as when cooking a jacket potato in about 6 minutes, or minimal, for example in the case of rice and pasta, but the additional benefit is being able to cook foods with the minimum attention and to just the right degree, be it *al dente*, tender-crisp, fork-tender or succulently moist.

ADVANTAGES OF MICROWAVE COOKING

Speed
You can reduce normal cooking times by up to 75 per cent by using a microwave oven.

Nutrient Retention
Nutrient loss from food is often associated with other cooking methods. With microwave cooking, since timings are short and so precise, and additional cooking liquid is minimal, there is less likely to be a loss of nutrients during cooking or by seepage as when boiling.

Economy
Since microwave cooking does not involve a lengthy preheating period and cooks for a shorter period of time, this method requires less energy and therefore saves money on energy bills.

Few Cooking Smells
Cooking odours are usually contained within the microwave oven cavity, so kitchen odours are kept to an absolute minimum.

Cool Kitchen
Because of the mechanics of microwave cooking, the microwave oven, dishes and the kitchen all stay cool, while only the food becomes piping hot. Also, in kitchens where there is a problem with ventilation, the microwave is a great improvement on the conventional hob, which creates a lot of steam during boiling or other moist cooking methods.

Less Risk of Burns
Since dishes do not become red hot, but only heat up by the conduction of heat from the food, there is less risk of getting a nasty

burn from dishes or from the oven itself. This makes the microwave one of the safest cooking machines for the very young and for the elderly or infirm to use.

Less Cleaning and Washing Up

It is possible to cook and serve in the same container with microwave cooking, thereby reducing the amount of washing up. Cleaning the cooker is also easier as food does not bake on or splatter as found in conventional ovens and on hobs.

An End to Dried-out Dinners

With a microwave oven, dried-out dinners can become a thing of the past. Individual members of the family can eat when they want and late-comers can have a meal reheated in minutes to just-cooked perfection.

SELECTING FOOD FOR MICROWAVE COOKING

Apart from a few restrictions, virtually any food can be cooked in the microwave, but there are some foods that cook better than others. When planning a meal or choosing a recipe consider the following:

Fish and Shellfish

Whether fresh or frozen, whole or filleted, plain cooked or in a fancy sauce, microwave-cooked fish and shellfish are hard to beat for texture, flavour, appearance and ease of preparation. With little fear of drying out, these delicate foods stay succulently moist. Often, the only additional ingredients required are a tablespoon or two of water, lemon juice or stock, or a little butter, so fish and seafood are favourites with those following a healthy diet regime or watching their weight.

Whole Fish Slit the skin in two or three places on whole fish, such as salmon, trout and mackerel, to prevent it from bursting during cooking. (Boil-in-the-bag prepared fish should also have the pouch pierced.) The narrow end of the tail may need protecting for half the cooking time by shielding with a little foil.

Fillets, Steaks and Portions For best results when cooking fillets, roll them up into an even shape and secure each one with a wooden cocktail stick. Brush with lemon juice or melted butter and cover tightly during cooking. Fish steaks and pieces should be cooked so that the thicker portions are to the outer edge of the dish and the thinner pieces to the centre, where they receive the least microwave energy.

Coated Portions Breadcrumb-coated and battered fish can be cooked in the microwave, but the result will not be as crisp as when cooked conventionally. A microwave browning dish may help appreciably with these products.

Shellfish Prawns, shrimps, lobster and scallops cook superbly, but always start with the minimum time when cooking these items as they cook very quickly; also remember to take the standing time into account as part of the overall cooking process. Mussels and clams can also be steamed and cooked in the microwave with unbelievable ease.

Poultry and Game

Whole birds; quarters; breast, thigh and drumstick portions; stir-fry strips; and medallions of poultry and game can be cooked in the microwave with good results. Those dishes that require little browning, with portions cooked in a sauce, are most successful.

Whole Birds Truss well to hold the wings and legs close to the body to give a neat, compact shape. The narrow wing tips and drumstick bone ends may have to be protected with small pieces of foil for part of the cooking time. Start cooking whole birds breast-side down and turn over halfway through cooking. Place on a special microwaveproof roasting rack or on an upturned saucer so that the bird is lifted above the cooking juices.

With large birds and longer cooking times, browning is usually sufficient, but smaller birds and portions may need a little help. In all cases, whether cooking a whole bird or portions, these can be browned under a preheated hot grill after microwave cooking – the time savings are still considerable and warrant microwave cooking.

When cooking birds that have been stuffed, add an extra 1 minute per 450g/1lb to the times recommended in cooking charts. After cooking, leave to stand, covered in a tent of foil, to make best use of the residual heat; you will also find that the bird is easier to carve.

Small Birds and Portions Small birds, chicken quarters and small poultry joints should be cooked skin-side up, with the thicker parts towards the outside of the dish. Many will brown and crisp more readily if placed in a roasting bag.

If you are unsure of timings, then consider investing in a microwave thermometer, which takes the guesswork out of roasting and cooking times by indicating the internal temperature of the food.

Meat

With careful consideration of the quality and cut, meat cooked in the microwave is a great success. Cheaper, longer-cooking cuts can be microwaved with a measure of success, but the microwave performs better with prime-quality cuts. With the exception of roast pork, do not salt meat before microwave cooking as this draws out the moisture and toughens the meat.

Joints Ideally, choose joints that are symmetrically shaped; in other words, bone and roll joints like legs and shoulders for perfect results.

Minced Meat Minced beef, lamb and pork cook magnificently, whether as burgers or in moist dishes, like chilli con carne or Bolognese sauce. Meatloaves should be made in a ring mould for faster cooking.

Cubed Meat Cubes of meat for dishes such as casseroles, hot pots and curries, should be cut into pieces of the same size to ensure even cooking. Reduce the liquid required for such dishes by up to a third as there is very little evaporation in microwave cooking. Vegetables in casserole-type dishes tend to retain their shape and do not break down to thicken the liquid.

Sausages, Bacon and Kebabs Sausages, bacon and other fatty meats cook quickly with some degree of browning, but cover them with a sheet of absorbent kitchen paper during cooking to prevent fat from splattering on the oven walls. Wooden skewers should be used for kebabs which should, ideally, be cooked on a microwave roasting rack or placed across a shallow microwaveproof dish for success.

Vegetables

Whether freshly harvested from your garden, bought in the market, plucked from the supermarket shelf or taken from the freezer or store cupboard, the microwave will cook your vegetable selection to perfection. Only the minimum amount of water is used for most vegetables, so results are temptingly colourful and tender-crisp. Season with salt after cooking, as salt sprinkled directly on to vegetables can cause them to dehydrate and toughen.

Whole Vegetables Potatoes, aubergines and tomatoes need pricking before cooking to prevent them from bursting. Jacket potatoes will also have a crisper, drier skin if cooked on a sheet of absorbent kitchen paper. Whole vegetables or items which are not cut into small pieces should be positioned so that thicker parts are towards the outer edge of the dish, where they receive the most energy.

Cut Vegetables Most vegetables should be cut into uniformly sized pieces and placed in a cook bag or covered dish. Stir, rearrange or shake the vegetables halfway through the cooking time to ensure even results.

Fruit

From the basic apple to the exotic mango, fruit can be cooked in the microwave to retain its glorious characteristics. Most fruits can be prepared, sprinkled with sugar and cooked in a roasting bag or dish in the same way as fresh vegetables. Other items can be baked whole, poached in wine, cider or syrup, or stuffed with a sweetened filling.

Whole Fruit These must be scored or pricked if they are not peeled, so that the skin does not burst during cooking. Careful timing is important as fruit cooks surprisingly quickly.

Dried Fruit Dried fruit mixtures can also be cooked quickly to make fruit salads, compôtes and crumbles. Try mixtures of dried apple, pear, mango, peach, apricot and prune, and cook them in fruit juice and water for mouth-watering puddings at any time of the year.

Frozen Fruit The microwave is also useful for preparing fruit for the freezer when there is a glut, good price at the market or windfall of tree fruit. Use the microwave for cooking the fruit or for speedily making the sugar syrup in which to freeze fruit for long-term storage.

Pasta, Rice, Grains and Pulses

Any healthy diet should have its fair share of pasta, rice, grains and pulses; but, so often, it is the lengthy preparation of the latter that prevents us from serving them more often. The microwave makes light work of rehydrating beans and pulses, reducing what was once a long, overnight process of soaking to about 1½ hours.

The time savings with cooking pasta, rice, grains and pulses are virtually negligible but the bonuses are that little or no attention is required during cooking; the results are superb; there is no sticky, tacky saucepan to wash afterwards; no steamy kitchen and boil-over spills; and the food can be cooked ahead and reheated to perfection later.

All About Microwaves

For centuries people have cooked food to make it more palatable, easier to digest and safe to eat. From the smoky fire of prehistoric times through to today's high-tech microwave ovens, the principle of heating food to cook it has remained the same; the difference is in the speed of cooking and the methods employed. Traditional methods of cooking food in the fire, in the gas or electric oven and under or over the charcoal grill use conduction as the prime method of introducing heat, but what are microwaves and how do they cook?

MICROWAVE COOKING MADE SIMPLE

The mechanics of microwave cooking are no more magical than a television or radio. Inside the microwave is a magnetron vacuum tube, the "heart" or "brains" of the microwave, which converts ordinary household electrical energy into high-frequency electro-magnetic waves, called microwaves. The microwaves are then directed into the oven cavity, through a wave guide, and stirred by a fan for even distribution.

MICROWAVES IN ACTION

The waves are either reflected, pass through some materials or are absorbed by other materials. Metals reflect them (so cooking utensils must be non-metallic); glass, pottery, china, paper and most plastics allow them to pass through (so they make ideal cooking utensils); and foods absorb them.

The microwaves are absorbed by the moisture in food, causing the food molecules to vibrate rapidly, thus producing heat to cook food.

Imagine the boy scout rubbing two twigs together to light a fire and you have the general idea. However, the speed at which the microwaves cause the molecules to vibrate is millions of times per second, producing remarkably intense heat that cooks super fast.

This is completely different from conventional methods, where heat is passed along a chain from one molecule to the next until the whole becomes hot and cooked. It is especially different in that dishes remain cool, metals cannot be used and timings are fast, calling for different cooking procedures and techniques.

FACTORS WHICH AFFECT MICROWAVE COOKING

Starting Temperature of Food

Foods that are cooked from room temperature will take less time to cook than foods that are frozen or chilled. Cooking times in the recipes that follow are based on starting temperatures at which the foods are normally stored, unless otherwise stated.

Density of Food

The denser the food, the longer it takes to cook. Heavy, dense foods, like potatoes, will take longer to cook than light porous foods, like sponge cakes. For the same reason a solid, dense mass of food, like a whole cauliflower, will take longer to cook than the same food divided into pieces (in the case of cauliflower, cut into small florets) and spread out for cooking.

Composition of Food

Foods which are high in fats and sugars will cook faster than foods high in liquid because fats and sugars absorb microwave energy more readily. They also reach higher temperatures during the cooking process than water-based foods. It therefore takes longer to cook foods that are high in moisture, like vegetables, than it does to cook those with little moisture, such as breads and cakes.

Quantity of Food

As the volume or quantity of food being cooked in the microwave increases, the cooking time increases. If you double the amount of food, the time will increase by about half as much again.

Size and Shape of Food

Smaller pieces of food will cook more quickly than larger pieces and uniformly shaped pieces cook more evenly than irregular-shaped items. Cutting foods into regular pieces, fingers or rounds and slicing meat across the grain prior to cooking will all help to ensure even cooking. With unevenly shaped pieces that cannot be cut, the thinner parts will cook faster than the thicker areas and they should be placed towards the centre of the dish where they can be grouped together to receive less energy. Ideally, portions of food that are of the same size and shape cook most evenly.

It is also important to remember that round and ring shapes cook more evenly than square, oval or rectangular shapes. With the latter, there is a concentration of energy in the corners and at the ends that can cause charring; to avoid this, protect the corners with small pieces of smooth foil to shield them from the microwave energy.

Bones in Meat

Bones in meat conduct heat, therefore meat next to the bone in a joint will cook first. Wherever possible, it is wise to bone and roll meat for even cooking. If not, then remember to shield thin areas of meat next to the bone halfway through the cooking time to prevent overcooking.

Height in the Oven

Areas that are closest to any source of energy cook faster than those further away, and the microwave is no exception to this rule. Depending on its design, your microwave may cook faster near the floor or the roof, where the energy source is located. Rotating, turning over and stirring foods will minimize this effect.

THE MICROWAVE COOKER

All basic models are much the same in design: they consist of a cabinet, magnetron, wave guide, wave stirrer, power supply, power cord and controls. Some have special extra features such as automatic defrost, variable power control, turntable, integral ther-mometer or temperature probe, browning or crisping elements and stay-hot devices.

The microwaves are safely contained in the cavity by the metal lining inside the base and walls, which reflects the microwaves into the food. All cooker doors and frames are fitted with special seals as an extra safety measure to ensure that the microwaves stay in the cooker. In addition, all microwave cookers have one or more cut-out devices so that the flow of microwaves stops automatically whenever the door is opened or if the door has not been shut properly or is damaged.

Many portable microwave cookers have a turntable, which means that foods, such as fish, do not need turning.

Portable Microwave Cookers

These are undoubtedly the most popular. Almost as light and certainly as portable as a television, they require a 13 or 15 amp plug for use, making such cooking machines popular choices for students, flat-dwellers and the elderly. They are also good for use in a boat, caravan or second home.

A portable microwave may be sited conveniently on a work top, trolley or other firm, stable surface. Some models, with very basic controls, have been developed for the 'simplistic cooking and reheating' market, and are usually short in height, designed to fit under the work surface. Often budget-priced, this type of microwave will accom-modate a chicken or a couple of stacked plated meals, but it is not suitable for those who require a flexible oven arrangement or sophisticated cooking.

Double Oven Cooker

A few microwave models are available in the same unit as a conventional cooker, with the microwave acting as a second or double oven. Most models are built-in, but a few free-standing models are available.

Combination Cookers

This is an expanding section of the microwave market and one that is likely to attract second-time buyers. These cookers have the facility to cook by both microwave and conventional means in one single operation and in one unit. The conventional and microwave powers can operate separately, simultaneously or in sequence, as required. Some models also offer further choice, with fan-assisted ovens, grills or automatic cooking sequence controls for microwave, combination and conventional cooking. In the chapters that follow, look out for recipes that can be cooked using combination controls, but follow the timings given in your manufacturer's instruction booklet.

Installing the Microwave

All that is required to install a portable microwave cooker is a fused power socket. Manufacturers also recommend that you place the microwave on a stable surface and have adequate ventilation. It is therefore possible to site the microwave in a multitude of places – the kitchen work surface is typical, but also consider a trolley that can be wheeled between rooms or even out on to the terrace or patio for outdoor dining, providing wonderful flexibility when preparing accompaniments for barbecues.

If you plan to build-in your microwave, then ensure that you buy the correct fixing kit or housing unit, with adequate venting, and always check your microwave handbook for any special instructions.

Cleaning the Microwave

This is something of a bonus! Since the walls in the microwave oven cavity remain cool during cooking, cleaning is often just a quick-wipe operation. Food does not have the opportunity to bake-on, so wiping the inside at regular intervals, or when spills occur, with a damp, soapy cloth is sufficient. Remember always to disconnect the oven from the electrical supply before wiping or cleaning. Remove and wash oven trays, shelving and bases according to the manufacturer's instructions.

Wipe the outside surfaces and door regularly, but do not allow water to seep into the vents. If necessary, also clean any air filters or the stirrer fan guard according to the manufacturer's instructions.

Stale cooking smells can be removed by boiling a solution of 1 part lemon juice to 3 parts water in a microwaveproof bowl in the microwave for about 5 minutes on HIGH. Then wipe the oven cavity dry with a clean cloth.

Servicing

Remember to have the microwave checked by a qualified engineer every 12 months, or as recommended by the manufacturer.

NOTE
Do not operate the microwave oven when it is empty. For safety, especially when young children are around, place a cup of water in the cooker when it is not in use. If the cooker is accidentally switched on, the water will absorb the energy, then there is negligible risk of damaging the magnetron, something that can occur if the oven is operated when empty.

A sophisticated microwave cooker with combination cooking facility.

Microwave Dishes and Utensils

Without doubt, the range of dishes and utensils that can be used in the microwave is wider than that for cooking conventionally.

GLASS, POTTERY AND CHINA

Ovenproof and plain glass, pottery and china are all suitable for microwave cooking. Be sure to check that they do not have any metallic trim, screws or handles and, if using a pottery dish, that it is non-porous.

Clear glass dishes, such as Pyrex, are particularly useful since you can actually see the food being cooked and check its progress during cooking.

Glass measuring jugs are also superb and allow you to measure, mix, cook and, sometimes, serve from the same container. Ovenproof glass and glass-ceramic dishes are invaluable for use in one operation from the freezer to the microwave and vice versa (once the food has cooled completely).

The only type of glass to avoid for microwave cooking is the leaded type most often found as decorative drinking glassware.

PAPER

Paper is a good utensil for low heat and short cooking times, such as thawing, reheating or very short cooking, and for foods with a low fat, sugar or water content. Napkins, absorbent kitchen paper, cups, cartons, paper freezer wrap and the paper pulp board often used for supermarket packaging are all suitable. Absorbent kitchen paper or paper towels are especially useful for cooking fatty foods, since they absorb excess fats and oils and can be used to prevent splattering on the oven walls.

Avoid using metal in any form, including dishes wth metal decoration or trims; porous pottery and mugs or cups with glued-on handles; crystal glass; and polystyrene trays or non-dishwasher-safe plastics.

Wax-coated paper cups and plates should be avoided since the high temperature of the food will cause the wax to melt; they can be used for thawing items to be served cold, like frozen cakes and desserts.

PLASTICS

Whether these are dishwasher safe or not provides a useful indication as to whether or not a plastic item is suitable for microwave use. Unless made of a thermoplastic material, plastic dishes and containers should not be used for cooking foods with a high fat or sugar content, since the heat of the food may cause the plastic to melt and lose its shape.

Plastic or clear film for microwave use and items like bags suitable for boil-in-the-bag cooking work well.

Pierce a bag or film before cooking to allow steam to escape or fold back a corner to vent the film and prevent it from ballooning during cooking. Also take extra special care when removing clear film or opening plastic bags in case any trapped steam escapes and burns the hand or forearm.

Roasting bags provide a clean, convenient way of cooking many foods, from vegetables to roasts. Roasts particularly benefit from their use since browning seems to take place more readily in a roasting bag. Either tie loosely with room for steam to escape or snip a couple of holes in the bag to aid the escape of steam and replace the metal ties with elastic, string or a non-metal tie.

Do not attempt to microwave in thin polythene bags as they will not withstand the heat of the food. Thicker storage or freezer bags are acceptable. Use elastic bands, string or non-metal ties to secure the bags loosely before cooking.

Melamine is not recommended for microwave cooking as it absorbs enough microwave energy to cause charring.

COTTON AND LINEN

Napkins are ideal for short warming or reheating procedures, such as reheating bread rolls for serving. It is important to use only cotton or linen, as synthetic fibres, or fabrics containing a proportion of them, will be damaged.

WOODEN BOWLS AND BAKEWARE

These are suitable only for short periods of reheating, otherwise the wood or wicker will tend to dry out, crack or char.

SPECIAL MICROWAVE EQUIPMENT

With the increased popularity of microwave cooking, there are many specialist innovations in microwave cookware. Several ranges manufactured from polythene, polystyrene and

A selection of everyday items that are useful for microwave cooking.

thermoplastics are now widely available and come in a comprehensive range of shapes and sizes. If you are an enthusiastic microwave cook then you might consider investing in some of the more useful items such as a microwave baking tray, roasting rack, bun or muffin tray, ring mould and whisk.

If the microwave is your only form of cooker, you may well be interested in some other very special items of cookware, developed to broaden the options when cooking in a microwave. These include a special popcorn cooker, a microwave pressure cooker, special kebab and burger or chop cooker, and a range of microwaveproof saucepans.

Thermometers
Thermometers made specially for microwave ovens are available but can be used in an oven only when specified by the oven's manufacturer. Their main use is for checking the internal temperature of a meat roast to ensure it is cooked to your requirements. They can also be used to check that, after cooking for the recommended time, the internal

temperature of ready-made meals is sufficiently high to destroy microorganisms which may be present and could cause food poisoning. Some newer ovens have an automatic cooking control based on a temperature-sensing probe that can be inserted into the food while in the oven. When the food reaches a precise temperature, the oven turns itself off automatically.

Browning Dishes
Available from most microwave dealers and large kitchenware stores, these duplicate the browning and searing processes of conventional cooking. Especially useful for pre-browning burgers, chops, sausages and steaks, they can also be used to 'fry' eggs and sandwiches, and to brown vegetables.

The browning dish is made of a glass ceramic substance with a special coating that absorbs microwave energy. It is preheated in the microwave until the base coating changes colour, usually for about 8 minutes on HIGH. Always follow specific manufacturer's instructions as dishes, coatings and timings vary.

Examples of special microwave cookware.

The food is then placed on the dish to brown and turned to sear both sides. Preheating times and browning or searing times differ according to the food being cooked and the power output of the oven. Always follow the manufacturer's instructions for best results.

Checking Suitability for Microwave Cooking

If you intend to cook food in both the microwave and the conven-tional oven in a continuous operation, be sure to use a dish that is ovenproof as well as microwaveproof. The following is a simple test to check microwave suitability.

Fill a heatproof cup with cold water and stand it in the utensil being checked. Place the utensil in the microwave and microwave on HIGH for 1¼ minutes. If the water is warm in the cup and the utensil is cool, go ahead and use the utensil. If the utensil is warm or even hot and the water is still cool, or barely lukewarm, do not use the utensil for microwave cooking.

The Shape and Size of Dish to Use

After checking the material, consider the shape and size of the dish or utensil. Ideally, the more regular the shape the better for microwave cooking. For example, a round shape is much better than an oval; a straight-sided container is better than a curved one as the microwaves can penetrate more evenly; and a large shallow dish is better than a small deep one as the food is spread over a greater surface area and therefore exposed to more microwave energy.

A Few Ideas
The following novel pieces of cookware can be used in the microwave successfully:
• scallop shells
• glass or plastic baby bottles for warming milk and juice
• wooden toothpicks for securing foods and wooden kebab skewers for brochettes and kebabs
• paper bun cases for buns and muffins – support them in teacups or ramekin dishes.

Material to Avoid – Metals

Most manufacturers object to the use of metal. Even small amounts in the oven will reflect the microwaves so that they do not penetrate the food to be cooked.

Therefore, avoid metal dishes, baking trays and metal baking tins, foil dishes, cast-iron cookware, plates and china trimmed with a metallic design, metal kebab skewers, any dish with a metal screw or attachment and the paper-coated metal ties often found with freezer and cook bags.

Microwave Techniques

PREPARING INGREDIENTS

When cutting ingredients, prepare even-sized pieces so that they cook at the same rate.

• Slim strips of vegetables, such as carrots, cook more quickly and evenly than large, irregular pieces or different-sized whole vegetables.

• Even cubes or dice cook well. Large vegetables, such as swede, turnip, potato or pumpkin can all be cut into neat cubes to promote quick, even cooking.

• Slicing meat across the grain into thin pieces helps to tenderize it.

SCORING OR PRICKING FOODS

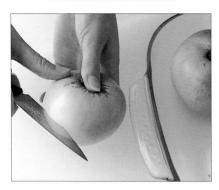

Foods with tight skins or membranes, such as sausages, kidneys, giblets, whole fish, jacket potatoes, egg yolks and apples must be lightly pricked or scored prior to cooking or they are liable to burst or explode. This is because of the tremendous amount of pressure that develops within foods that cook very quickly.

STIRRING

Stirring is important when cooking conventionally, and it is also necessary when cooking by microwave. Conventionally, we stir to redistribute heat from the bottom of the pan to the top, but with a microwave the aim is to redistribute heat and cooked areas from the outside to the centre of a dish for even cooking. Precise stirring instructions will be given in a recipe if it is important; if not, stirring halfway through cooking is usually sufficient.

ROTATING

If your microwave has a turntable, then this cooking technique becomes redundant. In models without a turntable, a quarter or half turn of the dish at regular intervals during the cooking period will ensure even results when food cannot be stirred or turned over.

TURNING OVER

Many large or dense items of food, such as potatoes or chicken drumsticks, should be turned over about halfway through cooking to ensure good results.

COOK'S TIP

A pair of food tongs is useful for turning firm foods, such as chicken portions, chops and sausages, for example.

ARRANGING FOOD

Arranging foods carefully in a dish for microwave cooking can mean that an ingredient is perfectly cooked rather than merely adequately cooked. For success, follow these guidelines.

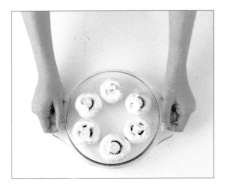

• Try to cook foods of an even or similar size together and, if possible, arrange them in a ring pattern in a dish, leaving the centre empty.

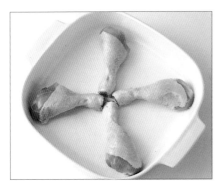

• If foods are of an irregular shape, like chicken drumsticks or spears of broccoli, then arrange the thicker sections to the outside of the dish in a spoke-like arrangement so that the thick areas will receive the most energy and cook more quickly than the thin areas that are grouped together.

• Arrange whole fish in pairs, head to tail, to form an even area that will cook uniformly. Thin areas cook more quickly than thick or large areas, which are not penetrated as quickly by microwaves.

• When reheating plated meals, ensure food is spread out evenly. Thicker vegetables should be arranged towards the edge to receive the most energy.

• When heating more than one plated meal at a time, special plastic microwave stacking rings can be placed between plates. These rings ensure plates are positioned so that they all receive an equal amount of energy and therefore the meals reheat at the same rate.

• Try to ensure that the depth of food is even; if it is not, stir or rearrange ingredients.

• Foods cooked in a ring pattern or mould make the most of the microwave. Cakes cook particularly well in a ring mould. If you don't have one, then improvise: place a glass tumbler in a round microwaveproof dish, and hold it in place while adding the mixture.

REARRANGING FOODS

Even with a turntable, rearranging foods (usually once) will ensure even results. Move foods from the outside of the dish to the centre and vice versa.

• Rearrange foods cooked in a bag by gently shaking the bag. Remember that scalding-hot steam can escape as the contents of the bag are shuffled, so protect your hand and forearm with a folded dish towel or oven glove.

SHIELDING

As with conventional baking, some parts of foods are more vulnerable to overcooking than others. In such cases, it is acceptable to use small smooth strips of foil to protect thin or vulnerable areas.

This is the only time when metal may be introduced into a typical microwave oven, and it is important to make sure it does not touch the oven walls. Position the foil on the food for about half the cooking time, securing small patches with wooden cocktail sticks, if necessary.

Check the manufacturer's handbook to ensure that this is permissible in your particular model of microwave oven.

• Fish heads and tails should be protected to prevent eyes from bursting and thin areas from overcooking.

• Wing tips on poultry and the thinner tail-ends on ducks should be shielded to prevent them from overcooking and drying out.

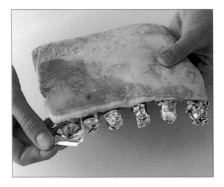

• Protruding bones, for example as on a rack of lamb, should be shielded to prevent scorching.

• Narrow ends of joints of meat, such as at the end of a leg of lamb or pork, should be shielded.

COVERING AND WRAPPING

Problems of surfaces drying out, splattering of food on the cavity walls and slower-than-optimum cooking times can all be eliminated by covering or wrapping foods. This locks in moisture, retains juices and speeds up cooking by trapping heat-retaining steam.

• Use double-strength plastic cooking bags, suitable for boiling

(sometimes referred to as "boil-in-the-bag" bags or "cook bags") or roasting bags for vegetables, meat and poultry. Replace metal ties with elastic bands.

• Some bags come with special, microwaveproof plastic clips.

• String can be used to loosely tie bags closed.

COOK'S TIP

Remember to ensure that a cooking bag is not too hot to hold before picking it up; protect your hand with a folded dish towel, if necessary, and be aware that scalding-hot steam may escape from any small opening at the top of the bag as the contents move when lifted or as they are being rearranged.

• Use a tight-fitting purpose-made lid or improvise by using a saucer or plate instead.

• Cover bowls with a tight membrane of microwave-safe clear film. Puncture the top to allow some steam to escape during cooking.

• Turn back a small area of clear film to provide a vent to prevent a ballooning effect during cooking. Take care when removing clear film, as it will trap a significant amount of scalding-hot steam even when it is vented.

• Greaseproof paper may be used to cover small bowls, for example as when cooking steamed puddings. The paper may be secured with a large elastic band.

• Use absorbent kitchen paper as a base on which to stand food.

• Absorbent kitchen paper can also be used as a cover for some foods. It is especially good for absorbing excess moisture given off by foods like potatoes and bread.

• Covering bacon with absorbent kitchen paper prevents spattering as well as ensuring that moisture that is given off is absorbed.

• Absorbent kitchen paper is also invaluable for drying herbs.

• When dampened, absorbent kitchen paper can be used for reheating and steaming pancakes and shellfish.

COOK'S TIP

Even though microwave cooking is a moist method, foods can dry out because of the speed with which moisture evaporates from them. Microwave-safe clear film is often the most practical choice of covering, allowing you to see what's happening in the dish. When folded back at one corner, the contents can be stirred during cooking without discarding the film. Always remove the film starting at the side furthest away from you to avoid scalding your hands or forearms.

REMOVING EXCESS COOKING JUICES

Any juices that seep from food will absorb microwave energy. If these juices are considerable, and the cooking time is longer than about 5 minutes on HIGH, it is advisable to remove some liquid regularly during cooking. Excess juices can prolong the cooking time appreciably. The juices can always be replaced towards the end of the cooking time if the food starts to dry out too much. Examples include cooking a chicken, duck or turkey.

OBSERVING STANDING TIMES

Food continues to cook by conduction after the microwave energy has been turned off. This is not solely a feature of microwave cooking – the same applies to a lesser degree with conventional cooking. With microwave cooking there is greater residual heat, so it is important to err on the side of safety and undercook rather than overcook food. Whereas there is no rescue package for overcooked food, additional cooking time can always be given if the dish is still inadequately cooked after observing the standing time.

BROWNING FOODS

As a result of little applied surface heat during rapid cooking, foods cooked in the microwave do not readily brown. Try the following tips to encourage browning or disguise any pale results.

• Grill foods like gratins and roasts before or after microwave cooking.

• Use a specialist microwave browning dish, especially for foods like chops, steaks, fried eggs, toasted sandwiches, stir-fries and chicken portions.

• Buy or make a browning mix to coat foods – paprika, toasted breadcrumbs, crushed crisps, soy sauce, Worcestershire sauce and soup mixes all work well.

• Due to its high fat content, bacon browns readily, so it can be laid over poultry or roast meat.

• Baked items, such as cakes, biscuits, breads and muffins, can be sprinkled or coated with toasted coconut, chocolate vermicelli, chopped nuts, chopped glacé fruits, poppy seeds, toasted seeds and dark-coloured spices.

• Glaze ham, poultry or game with fruit preserve, particularly redcurrant jelly or citrus marmalade, before cooking to add colour.

• Add icing or frosting to a pale cake or other baked items after cooking.

Herby Baked Tomatoes are cooked in the microwave, then browned under the grill.

The Microwave and Freezer

During its introductory years, the domestic microwave was often referred to as "the unfreezer" due to its ability to defrost food both quickly and efficiently, and this is still one of the major advantages of microwave ownership.

Capitalizing on this effect, almost all microwave manufacturers have introduced a special DEFROST control or button to ensure optimum defrosting microwave action. This control programmes the microwave to introduce just the right amount of energy to defrost food without cooking it. This is done by pulsing the power on and off at regular intervals over a period of time.

When a defrost setting is not built in, it is possible to simulate the action of the setting by turning the microwave on and off manually at regular intervals, allowing rest periods in between; but this is rarely as successful as using a pre-programmed setting and it can be time-consuming.

DEFROSTING TIPS

Refer to your own manufacturer's handbook for a guide to defrosting times, but always err on the side of safety by heating for too short a period, rather than too long, until you can readily judge the defrosting speed of your own particular type of microwave.

• Open all cartons and remove any metal lids, ties or fastenings before defrosting food.

• Defrost foods slowly. Never try to hurry the process as there is the danger of overcooking the food or drying it out unnecessarily.

• Frozen foods wrapped in foil or placed in foil containers should have all foil removed, and they should be placed in a suitable dish for the microwave.

• Turn foods over during defrosting, about halfway through the recommended time.

• If it is not possible to turn food over during defrosting (for example, as with a decorated cake), then rotate the item or container regularly for even defrosting.

• Flex any pouches of food that cannot be broken up or stirred during the defrosting time and rotate on a regular basis.

• Place foods like cakes, bread rolls and pastry items on a double sheet of absorbent kitchen paper to absorb excess moisture that could cause the food to become soggy.

• Blocks of frozen food should be broken up with a fork during defrosting so that frozen chunks receive the maximum amount of microwave energy.

• Separate any blocks of frozen meat items, such as hamburgers, steaks, chops and sausages, as they defrost.

• Remove any giblets from the cavity of a chicken and other poultry or game birds as soon as they have defrosted.

• Remove any juices or drips from frozen foods during the defrosting time with a bulb baster or spoon as these will only continue to absorb microwave energy, leaving less to defrost the main food.

• Items like meat joints, whole birds and whole fish should be defrosted until icy, then left to defrost completely at room temperature before cooking.

• If any parts of the food start to defrost too fast (or even begin to become warm or cook), shield or protect these areas with small strips of smooth foil. These can be attached with wooden cocktail sticks where necessary. Check that this is acceptable for your model of microwave by reading the manufacturer's instructions.

• Always observe standing times as foods will continue to thaw by means of conduction from the small level of internal heat that is produced. Allow foods to defrost until they are just icy.

• Before defrosting, prick, slash or vent membranes and skins. Also, pierce clear film, pouches or similar wrappings in the same way as when cooking food in a skin.

• If you intend to defrost and cook in one operation, then follow all the guidelines on stirring, turning, rotating and rearranging foods, not forgetting to allow standing time before serving.

> ### COOK'S TIP
> ❧
>
> If a member of your household is not a confident cook, but has to reheat an occasional meal, freeze suitable portions with a label giving brief instructions for defrosting and reheating the food in the microwave.

FREEZER TO MICROWAVE REMINDERS

The microwave and freezer are a terrific twosome to ease the life of the regular home cook, working mother, busy hostess and anyone with a prolific vegetable garden. When freezing home-made food that will later be defrosted or cooked in the microwave, the following hints are worth remembering.

• Freeze food in a microwaveproof container, so it can be defrosted, reheated or cooked straight from the freezer.

• Single portions are very useful in the freezer, allowing any member of the family to quickly and easily defrost and cook an individual meal at any time.

• Before freezing a conventionally made pizza, pie, flan or quiche, cut it into portions so that the required number of servings can be removed from the freezer as required, rather than having to defrost the whole item.

• Complete cooked main courses can be plated on microwaveproof plates and frozen for almost instant dinners. Remember to follow the advice on arranging food for microwave cooking and reheating when preparing complete meals. Adding a sauce of some kind helps to keep the meal succulent and moist during defrosting and reheating.

• When cooking a main course, consider doubling the quantities and freezing the second meal for future use.

• Save time and effort in the future by freezing soups, casseroles and hot pots in freezerproof bags that are also suitable for microwave defrosting. Use large bags and knot the tops firmly to prevent the contents from leaking, and avoid using metal ties. The unopened bags can be placed in the microwave until the contents are slightly defrosted and free of the plastic, then the food is ready to be transferred to a suitable microwaveproof serving dish for the final reheating.

• Consider freezing home-grown or bargain vegetable produce in freezer and microwaveproof boil-in-the-bags. These will serve as freezing, defrosting and cooking containers, without the need to transfer the contents at all before serving.

FREEZING FOOD TO FIT A DISH

1 If you do not want to lose the use of the dish while the food is in the freezer, line it with freezer film or foil, arrange the food in the dish and then freeze.

2 Once frozen, turn the food out of the container, wrap it tightly, label and return to the freezer.

3 To defrost or reheat the food, remove the freezer film or foil and return the food to the original container before placing in the microwave.

COOKING AND FREEZING IN ONE BAG

1 Fruits like apples and pears can be cooked in a roasting bag or boilable bag.

2 When cooked, the fruit can be crushed in the bag to make a purée and sealed while still hot. As the mixture cools it will form a vacuum pack that is ideal for freezing and ready for defrosting or reheating in the microwave.

COOK'S TIP
Make a note of the weight of vegetables or fruit on freezer labels so you can calculate the microwave cooking time easily for the whole bag.

FREEZING AND DEFROSTING BABY FOOD

• Leftovers from suitable meals can easily be puréed and frozen in ice cube trays ready for baby and toddler meals. To defrost and reheat 2 cubes (about 60ml/4 tbsp food), place in a microwaveproof bowl. Place a small glass or cup of water in the microwave at the same time to absorb some energy and prevent the baby food from over-heating. Microwave on HIGH for 1–1¼ minutes until thawed and hot, stirring once to break up. Leave to stand and check the temperature before serving.

COOK'S TIP
Once the trays of baby food are frozen, release the hard cubes of purée and store them in an airtight polythene bag. This way you will not have all your ice cube trays in use.

REHEATING FOODS IN THE MICROWAVE

Most foods will reheat successfully in the microwave without loss of quality, flavour and colour, and with maximum nutrient retention compared to alternative reheating methods. For best results follow these guidelines.

• Arrange foods on a plate with the thicker portions to the outer edge where they will receive the most energy.

• When plating meals for reheating, try to arrange the food in an even layer.

• Cover foods with clear film if a lid is not used to retain moisture.

• Observe the standing time to make maximum use of the microwave energy and to prevent the food overcooking.

• When reheating potatoes, pastry items and other moist baked foods, place them on a double sheet of absorbent kitchen paper to absorb the excess moisture and prevent sogginess.

• If possible, stir foods regularly during reheating; if this is not possible, then turn foods over or rearrange them, or at least rotate the dish for even reheating.

Basic Recipes

The microwave is invaluable for cooking a host of dishes, as you will see from the recipes that follow in this book, and it is also indispensable for cooking a range of basic recipes that form the basis for more complicated dishes and meals. The following are a few of the most useful basic recipes.

GIBLET STOCK FOR GRAVY

1 Place the contents of a bag of giblets from a chicken, turkey or duck in a microwaveproof bowl with 300ml/½ pint/1¼ cups boiling water and a few sliced seasoning vegetables, such as carrots, celery and onion.

2 Microwave on HIGH for 7–10 minutes. Strain and use the gravy as required.

WHITE POURING SAUCE

1 Place 25g/1oz/2 tbsp butter in a microwaveproof jug and microwave on HIGH for 30–60 seconds, until melted.

2 Stir in 25g/1oz/2 tbsp plain flour and 300ml/½ pint/1¼ cups milk. Microwave on HIGH for 3½–4 minutes, stirring or whisking once every minute, until smooth, boiling and thickened. Season to taste and serve. Makes 300ml/½ pint/1¼ cups.

VARIATIONS

One-stage Sauce: Place the flour and butter in a microwaveproof jug, then add the milk and whisk lightly. The ingredients will not combine thoroughly at this stage as the butter does not mix in, but it will break into small pieces. Continue as above.

Caper Sauce: Add 15ml/1 tbsp drained capers and 5ml/1 tsp vinegar from the jar of capers or lemon juice to the cooked sauce. Good with cooked lamb.

Cheese Sauce: Add 50–115g/2–4oz grated cheese, a pinch of dry mustard powder and a pinch of cayenne pepper to the cooked sauce. Whisk or stir well. Serve with vegetables, eggs, fish or pasta.

Parsley Sauce: Add 15–30ml/ 1–2 tbsp chopped fresh parsley and a squeeze of lemon juice (optional) to the cooked sauce and whisk or stir well. Serve with fish, ham or bacon and vegetables.

SCRAMBLED EGGS

1 Place 15g/½oz/1 tbsp butter in a microwaveproof jug or bowl and microwave on HIGH for about 30 seconds to melt.

2 Beat 4 eggs with 30ml/2 tbsp milk and salt and pepper to taste. Add to the butter and microwave on HIGH for 1¼ minutes. Stir or whisk the set pieces of egg from the outside of the bowl or jug to the centre.

3 Microwave on HIGH for a further 1¼–1¾ minutes, stirring or whisking twice. When about three-quarters cooked, there is still a significant amount of runny egg, as shown here. When cooked, the eggs are moist, not completely set. Leave to stand for 1–2 minutes, by which time the eggs will be set ready for serving. Serves 2.

JACKET POTATOES

1 Scrub and prick the potatoes. Place on a double thickness of absorbent kitchen paper. If cooking more than two potatoes, arrange them in a ring pattern.

2 Microwave on HIGH for the time given, turning over halfway through cooking. Leave to stand for 3–4 minutes before serving.

3 The potatoes may be cut in half and the flesh forked up or mashed, then replaced in the shells, topped with cheese or butter and heated for a few seconds in the microwave to melt the butter or cheese before serving.

COOKING TIMES FOR JACKET POTATOES

1 x 175g/6oz	potato		4–6 minutes
2 x 175g/6oz	potatoes		6–8 minutes
3 x 175g/6oz	potatoes		8–12 minutes
4 x 175g/6oz	potatoes		12-15 minutes

CORN-ON-THE-COB

These can either be cooked husked or unhusked.

1 For fresh unhusked corn-on-the-cob, fold back the husk and discard the silk.

2 Replace the husk to cover the corn and arrange the cobs, evenly spaced, on the base of the cooker or turntable. Microwave on HIGH for the time given, rotating and rearranging once halfway through cooking. Leave to stand for 5 minutes before removing the husk and cutting off the woody base with a sharp knife.

3 Alternatively, wrap fresh husked cobs individually in clear film or place in a microwave-proof dish with 60ml/4 tbsp water and cover. Microwave on HIGH for the time given, rotating and rearranging once halfway through cooking. Leave to stand for 3–5 minutes before serving.

COOKING TIMES FOR CORN-ON-THE-COB

Cooking Times for Corn Cobs in Husks

1 x 175–225g/6–8oz	cob	3–5 minutes
2 x 175–225g/6–8oz	cobs	6–8 minutes
3 x 175–225g/6–8oz	cobs	8–10 minutes
4 x 175–225g/6–8oz	cobs	10–12 minutes

Cooking Times for Husked Corn Cobs

1 x 175–225g/6–8oz	cob	3–4 minutes
2 x 175–225g/6–8oz	cobs	5–6 minutes
3 x 175–225g/6–8oz	cobs	7–8 minutes
4 x 175–225g/6–8oz	cobs	9–10 minutes

HOLLANDAISE SAUCE

1 Place 115g/4oz/8 tbsp butter in a large microwaveproof jug and microwave on HIGH for 1½ minutes until melted. Whisk in 45ml/3 tbsp lemon juice, 2 egg yolks, a pinch of mustard powder and salt and pepper to taste.

2 Microwave on MEDIUM for 1 minute, whisk and serve. This sauce is delicious with poached salmon or cooked asparagus. Serves 4–6.

RED LENTILS

1 Place 225g/8oz/1 cup lentils in a large microwaveproof bowl. Add a little chopped onion, celery and lemon juice, if liked. Cover with 900ml/1½ pints/3¾ cups boiling water or stock and add salt and pepper to taste.

2 Cover, leaving a gap for steam to escape, and microwave on HIGH for 15–25 minutes, stirring once halfway through cooking. Time the cooking according to requirements: if you want the lentils to retain some shape, use the shorter time; if you want soft lentils for a soup or dip, use the longer cooking time. Serves 4.

QUICK SOAKING OF DRIED BEANS

1 To shorten the soaking time for dried beans, place them in a microwaveproof bowl and cover with boiling water.

2 Cover and microwave on HIGH for 5 minutes. Leave to stand for 1½ hours, then drain, rinse and cook the beans.

VEGETABLE RICE

1 Place 225g/8oz/generous 1 cup long grain white rice in a microwaveproof bowl with 550ml/18fl oz/scant 2½ cups boiling water, 5ml/1 tsp salt, and a knob of butter, if liked. Cover loosely with a lid or vented clear film and microwave on HIGH for 3 minutes.

2 Reduce the power setting to MEDIUM and microwave for a further 12 minutes, stirring two or three times.

3 Add 175g/6oz/about 1 cup diced and softened vegetables (for example a single vegetable or selection from peas, beans, peppers, onion and sweetcorn). Stir well to mix, cover and microwave on HIGH for 1½ minutes.

4 Leave to stand, tightly covered, for 5 minutes. Fluff the rice with a fork to separate the grains before serving. Serves 4.

PORRIDGE

1 Traditional and quick-cook varieties of porridge can be prepared quickly and easily in the microwave. To make traditional porridge, place 30g/1¼ oz/⅓ cup oatmeal in a microwaveproof bowl with 1.5ml/¼ tsp salt.

2 Stir in 175ml/6 fl oz/¾ cup water or milk, making sure that the oatmeal and liquid are thoroughly mixed.

3 Cover with vented clear film and microwave on LOW for 10–12 minutes, stirring twice. Leave to stand, covered, for 2 minutes before serving.

4 Prepare quick-cook oatmeal as above, but microwave on LOW for 5 minutes. Serves 1.

GARLIC OR HERB BREAD

1 Cut a 115g/4oz short, crusty French stick or Vienna loaf into diagonal slices about 4cm/1½in thick, almost to the base of the loaf but not quite through. Spread garlic or herb butter between the slices and re-form the loaf into a neat shape.

2 Wrap loosely in absorbent kitchen paper and microwave on HIGH for 1½ minutes. Serve at once, while still warm. Serves 4.

Making the Most of Your Microwave

Getting used to the speed of microwave cooking does take time, patience and perseverance, so you are unlikely to become a microwave mastercook overnight. The golden rule is to become a constant clock-watcher until you know your microwave really well. Do not be afraid or intimidated by the microwave – open the door, peer in and poke food as much as you like to see if it is defrosting, cooking or reheating adequately. You will soon be able to cook the recipes in this book successfully, adapt some of your own conventional favourites and halve or double quantities with practised ease.

The following are tips that will provide amusing, useful tricks to make you wonder how you ever managed without a microwave!

PEELING TOMATOES

Place up to 6 tomatoes in a ring on absorbent kitchen paper. Microwave on HIGH for 10–15 seconds. Leave to stand for 15 minutes, then peel the tomatoes.

PEELING PEACHES AND APRICOTS

Place up to 4 peaches in a microwaveproof bowl with very little water. Cover and microwave on HIGH for 1–1½ minutes. Leave the peaches to stand for 5 minutes, then drain and peel them.

TO SOFTEN CHILLED HARD CHEESES

Place about 225g/8oz chilled hard cheese on a microwaveproof serving plate and microwave on LOW for 30–34 seconds, turning over after half the time. Leave to stand for 5 minutes before serving.

TO RIPEN SEMI-SOFT CHEESE

Place about 225g/8oz semi-soft cheese on a microwaveproof serving dish and microwave on LOW for 15–45 seconds depending upon degree of ripeness, checking constantly and turning over after half of the time. Leave to stand for 5 minutes before serving.

SOFTENING BUTTER

Microwave on HIGH for 5–10 seconds, then leave to stand for 5 minutes before using.

BLANCHING ALMONDS

Place 250ml/8fl oz/1 cup water in a jug. Microwave on HIGH for 2½ minutes or until boiling, add the almonds and microwave for 30 seconds. Drain the nuts, then slip off their skins.

TOASTING NUTS

For a golden result, place in a browning dish and microwave on HIGH for 4–5 minutes, stirring each minute. Alternatively, for a lighter result, cook in an ordinary microwaveproof dish.

TOASTING COCONUT

Spread 115g/4oz/1 cup desiccated coconut on a microwaveproof plate. Microwave on HIGH for 5–6 minutes, stirring every 1 minute.

DRYING HERBS AND CITRUS RINDS

Place on a microwaveproof plate and microwave on HIGH until dry. Never leave unattended and check at 1 minute intervals to ensure success.

SQUEEZING CITRUS JUICE

To extract the maximum juice from citrus fruit, prick the skins and microwave on HIGH for 5–10 seconds.

TO DRY BREAD FOR CRUMBS

1 Place a thick slice of bread on a microwaveproof plate and microwave on HIGH for 2½–3½ minutes, until dry.

2 Allow the bread to cool completely before crumbling or grating it for use.

TO MAKE CROÛTONS

1 To make dry, oil-free croûtons, dice 175g/6oz bread into cubes. Place on kitchen paper on a large flat microwaveproof plate and microwave on HIGH for 3–4 minutes, stirring once every minute, until dry.

2 To make butter-crisp croûtons, place 25g/1oz/2 tbsp butter in a microwaveproof dish and microwave on HIGH for 30 seconds to melt.

3 Add 175g/6oz bread cubes and toss to coat them in the melted butter. Microwave on HIGH for 3–4 minutes, stirring every minute, until crisp and brown.

COOK'S TIP

Croûtons can be flavoured in a variety of ways to complement the dishes they garnish. A crushed garlic clove or a little dried oregano can be added to the butter for butter-crisp croûtons. Chopped fresh herbs, such as tarragon or parsley, should be tossed with the cooked croûtons. Grated Parmesan cheese or lemon rind can be added to cooked croûtons.

PROVING YEAST DOUGH

1 To rise bread dough quickly, give a 900g/2lb piece of dough short bursts of microwave energy on HIGH for 5–10 second intervals, observing a 10 minute standing time between each heating period.

2 Repeat until the dough has risen to double its size.

DEFROSTING FROZEN SHORTCRUST OR PUFF PASTRY

Place a 400g/14oz packet of pastry on a microwaveproof plate and microwave on DEFROST for 4–4½ minutes, turning over once during the time. Leave to stand for 5 minutes before using.

To Cook Poppadoms

1 Arrange two or three plain or spiced poppadoms on the base of the cooker or on the turntable so that they do not touch or overlap. Microwave on HIGH for 45–60 seconds until puffy and bubbling. Leave to stand on a wire rack for 15 seconds to crisp.

2 To make poppadom cases or cups (ideal for holding salad) position a poppadom over a small microwaveproof bowl and microwave on HIGH for 20–25 seconds. As it cooks, the poppadom will droop in folds over the bowl to make a cup shape. Leave to stand for about 15 seconds to crisp before removing from the bowl.

To Make Biscuit Cups

Ready-made biscuits, like brandy snaps and florentines, can be heated in the microwave over a microwaveproof bowl to form a cup shape that can later hold mousse, ice cream or fruit salad for an almost instant dessert. Position two biscuits over the top of two microwaveproof bowls and microwave on HIGH for 30–45 seconds, until very warm and pliable. While hot, mould the biscuits around the bowls to form cup shapes. Leave until completely cold and firm before removing from the bowls.

Softening Jams and Spreads

Remove any lids and any metal trims or transfer the jam or spread to a microwaveproof dish. Microwave on HIGH for about 5–10 seconds per 450g/1lb.

Dissolving Gelatine

1 Sprinkle the gelatine over cold water, as usual, and leave to stand until spongy.

2 Microwave on HIGH for 30 seconds until clear and completely dissolved.

Clarifying Crystallized Honey

Remove the lid and any metal trims on the jar. Microwave on HIGH for 1–2 minutes. Stir well.

Dissolving Jelly

1 Break up a 135g/4½oz jelly tablet and place in a microwaveproof bowl or jug with 150ml/¼ pint/⅔ cup water.

2 Microwave the jelly on HIGH for 2 minutes.

3 Stir well to dissolve, then make up with cold water according to the packet instructions.

MELTING CHOCOLATE

Break chocolate into pieces and place in a microwaveproof bowl. Microwave on HIGH, for about 1 minute per 25g/1oz.

SOFTENING ICE CREAM FOR SCOOPING

Microwave about 1 litre/ 1¾ pints/4 cups hard (not soft scoop) ice cream on MEDIUM for 45–90 seconds. Leave to stand for 1–2 minutes before scooping.

FLAMBÉING WITH ALCOHOL

Heat the alcohol, such as brandy, in a microwaveproof and flame-proof jug on HIGH for 15 seconds. It will then ignite more easily ready for pouring over Christmas pudding, pancakes or fresh fruit.

TO REHEAT READY-MADE FRESH BLACK COFFEE

Place 600ml/1 pint/2½ cups cold coffee in a microwaveproof jug and microwave on HIGH for 4½–5 minutes.

TO REHEAT A MUG OF TEA OR COFFEE

Make sure the mug is microwave-proof. Heat on HIGH for 30–60 seconds and stir before tasting. Repeat if necessary, always stirring before tasting as hot spots in the liquid can burn the mouth.

WARMING BABY'S BOTTLE

Invert the teat and microwave 250ml/8fl oz/1 cup prepared milk on HIGH for 1 minute to warm. Shake the bottle gently and test the milk to check the temperature before attempting to feed the baby. If in doubt check your baby milk formula instructions for preparing in the microwave.

TO HEAT MILK FOR DRINKS

Frothy hot milk for café au lait, hot chocolate or other beverages can be heated very quickly. Place 300ml/½ pint/1¼ cups cold milk in a microwaveproof jug and microwave on HIGH for 2–2½ minutes. Whisk well until frothy, if liked, and serve at once.

TO MAKE MULLED WINE

Mix 750ml/1¼ pints/3 cups red wine, 12 cloves, 2 small cinnamon sticks, the grated rind and juice of 1 orange and 1 lemon, and 30–45ml/2–3 tbsp brown sugar in a microwaveproof bowl or jug. Microwave on HIGH for 5 minutes, or until almost boiling. Add extra sugar to taste, if liked, and serve the wine warm. This serves about six.

Before You Begin

Microwave Powers and Settings

• All the recipes and charts in this book were created and tested using microwave ovens with a maximum power output of 650–700 watts.

• The ovens had variable power and the descriptions used refer to the following power outputs.

HIGH = 650–750 watts or 100%
MEDIUM HIGH = 500–550 watts or 75%
MEDIUM = 400 watts or 55–60%
LOW = 250 watts or 40%
DEFROST = 200 watts or 30%

• The chart below gives the approximate power input in watts at these levels and relative cooking times.

• The microwave ovens used for testing had turntables - if yours does not and tends to have an irregular heating pattern with hot and cold spots, then follow the rules on turning, rotating and rearranging foods.

• Metric measurements may vary from one recipe to another within the book, and it is essential to follow EITHER metric or Imperial. The recipes have been carefully balanced to get the very best results using only one set of measures and cannot be interchanged.

Unless Otherwise Stated

• eggs are size 3
• all spoon quantities are measured level

Foods to Avoid

The following foods do not cook well in the microwave and they are best avoided.

Eggs in Shells
These are liable to explode due to the build-up of pressure within the shell. Eggs can however be baked, scrambled, poached and "fried" in the microwave with superb results.

Popcorn
This can prove to be too dry to attract microwave energy, although some manufacturers have produced microwave popcorn, sold in a special bag with seasonings and flavourings, and this works superbly. A special microwave popcorn machine can also be purchased to cook ordinary popcorn in the microwave.

Batter-based and Some Air-incorporated Recipes
Items like Yorkshire pudding, soufflé, pancakes, choux pastry, batter-coated fish and whisked sponge mixtures need conventional cooking to become crisp and firm. The microwave will, however, make the basic sauce for a soufflé and will reheat pancakes perfectly.

Conventional Meringues
These should be cooked in the conventional oven since they do not dry sufficiently and become crisp in the microwave.

Deep-fat Frying
This is not recommended since it requires prolonged heating, it is difficult to control the temperature of the fat and the food may burn.

Liquid in Bottles and Pots
Check that bottles do not have necks that are too narrow to allow sufficient escape since steam as built-up pressure may cause them to shatter. Similarly, tall coffee pots, with slim spouts can break or cause coffee to spurt out.

Guide to Comparitive Microwave Oven Control Settings

Settings used in these recipes	Setting variations on popular microwave ovens				Approximate % power input	Approximate power outputs in watts	Cooking times in minutes – for times greater than 10 minutes simply add together the figures in the appropriate columns									
	1	keep warm	low	2	25%	150W	4	8	12	16	20	24	28	32	36	40
Defrost	2	simmer	simmer	3	30%	200W	3¼	6¾	10	13¼	16¾	20	26¼	26¼	30	33¼
Low	3	stew	medium/low	4	40%	250W	2½	5	7½	10	12½	15	17½	20	22½	25
	4	defrost	medium	5	50%	300W	2	4	6	8	10	12	14	16	18	20
Medium	5	bake	medium	6	60%	400W	1¾	3¾	5	6¾	8¼	10	12	13¼	15	16½
Medium High	6	roast	high	7–8	75%	500–600W	1¼	2¾	4	5¼	6¾	8	9¼	10¾	12	13¼
High	7	full/high	normal	10	100%	700W	1	2	3	4	5	6	7	8	9	10

SOUPS AND STARTERS

Chunky Bean and Vegetable Soup

A substantial soup, not unlike minestrone, using a selection of vegetables, with cannellini beans for extra protein and fibre. Serve with a hunk of wholegrain bread.

INGREDIENTS

Serves 4

30ml/2 tbsp olive oil

2 celery sticks, chopped

2 leeks, sliced

3 carrots, sliced

2 garlic cloves, crushed

400g/14oz can chopped tomatoes
  with basil

1.2 litres/2 pints/5 cups hot
  vegetable stock

425g/15oz can cannellini beans (or mixed
  pulses), drained

15ml/1 tbsp pesto sauce

salt and ground black pepper

shavings of Parmesan cheese, to serve

1 Place the olive oil in a large microwaveproof bowl with the celery, leeks, carrots and garlic. Microwave on HIGH for 4 minutes, stirring halfway through cooking, until softened.

2 Stir in the tomatoes and the stock. Cover and microwave on HIGH for 10 minutes, stirring halfway through cooking.

3 Stir in the beans and pesto, with salt and pepper to taste. Microwave on HIGH for a further 3–5 minutes, stirring halfway through cooking. Serve in heated bowls, sprinkled with shavings of Parmesan cheese.

COOK'S TIP

Canned chick-peas give the soup a delicious nutty flavour. Flageolet beans are more delicate and borlotti beans are slightly more substantial.

Italian Fish Soup

Serves 4

30ml/2 tbsp olive oil

1 onion, thinly sliced

a few saffron threads

5ml/1 tsp dried thyme

large pinch of cayenne pepper

2 garlic cloves, finely chopped

2 x 400g/14oz cans peeled tomatoes,
    drained and chopped

175ml/6fl oz/¾ cup dry white wine

1.85 litres/3¼ pints/8 cups hot fish stock

350g/12oz white, skinless fish fillets, cut
    into pieces

450g/1lb monkfish, membrane removed,
    cut into pieces

450g/1lb mussels in the shell,
    thoroughly scrubbed

225g/8oz small squid, cleaned and cut
    into rings

30ml/2 tbsp chopped fresh parsley

salt and ground black pepper

thickly sliced bread, to serve

1 Place the oil in a large microwaveproof bowl. Stir in the onion, saffron, thyme, cayenne pepper and salt to taste. Microwave on HIGH for 3 minutes, until soft. Add the garlic and microwave on HIGH for 1 minute.

2 Stir in the tomatoes, white wine and fish stock. Cover and microwave on HIGH for 10 minutes, stirring halfway through the cooking time.

3 Add the fish fillet and monkfish pieces to the bowl. Cover and microwave on HIGH for 2 minutes, stirring once.

4 Mix in the mussels and squid. Cover and microwave on HIGH for 2–3 minutes, stirring once, until the mussels open. Stir in the parsley and season with salt and pepper.

5 Ladle into warmed soup bowls and serve immediately, with warm crusty bread.

Creamy Cod Chowder

INGREDIENTS

Serves 4 – 6

350g/12oz smoked cod fillet

1 small onion, finely chopped

1 bay leaf

4 black peppercorns

900ml/1½ pints/3¾ cups skimmed milk

10ml/2 tsp cornflour

10ml/2 tsp water

200g/7oz canned sweetcorn kernels

l5ml/1 tbsp chopped fresh parsley

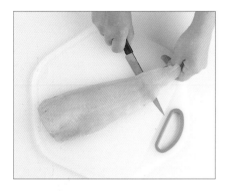

1 Skin the fish fillet. Hold the tail firmly and cut the fish off its skin using a sharp knife. Cut at an acute angle, taking care not to cut the skin and folding back the fish fillet.

2 Place the fish in a large microwaveproof bowl with the onion, bay leaf and peppercorns. Pour in the milk.

3 Cover and microwave on HIGH for 8–10 minutes, stirring twice, or until the fish is just cooked.

4 Using a slotted spoon, lift out the fish and flake it into large chunks. Remove and discard the bay leaf and peppercorns.

5 Blend the cornflour with the water and add to the milk mixture. Microwave on HIGH for 2–3 minutes, stirring twice, until slightly thickened.

6 Drain the sweetcorn kernels and add to the milk mixture with the flaked fish and parsley.

7 To reheat the chowder, microwave on HIGH for 2–3 minutes until piping hot, stirring twice, but do not boil. Ladle the chowder into four or six soup bowls and serve straight away.

Chilli Prawns

This delightful, spicy combination makes a tempting light main course for a casual supper. Serve with rice, noodles or freshly cooked pasta and a leafy salad.

INGREDIENTS

Serves 3–4

45ml/3 tbsp olive oil

2 shallots, chopped

2 garlic cloves, chopped

1 fresh red chilli, chopped

450g/1lb ripe tomatoes, peeled, seeded and chopped

15ml/1 tbsp tomato purée

1 bay leaf

1 thyme sprig

90ml/6 tbsp dry white wine

450g/1lb peeled cooked large prawns

salt and ground black pepper

roughly torn basil leaves, to garnish

1 Place the oil, shallots, garlic and chilli in a microwaveproof bowl and microwave on HIGH for 2 minutes, stirring once.

2 Add the tomatoes, tomato purée, bay leaf, thyme, wine and seasoning. Cover and microwave on HIGH for 6–7 minutes, stirring twice. Discard the herbs.

3 Stir the prawns into the sauce and microwave on HIGH for 2–3 minutes, stirring once. Taste and adjust the seasoning. Garnish with torn basil leaves and serve at once.

COOK'S TIP

For a milder flavour, scrape and then rinse out all the seeds from the chilli before chopping it.

Scallops with Ginger

Scallops cook very well in the microwave. Rich and creamy, this dish is very simple to make and quite delicious.

INGREDIENTS

Serves 4

40g/1½oz/3 tbsp butter

8–12 scallops, shelled

2.5cm/1in piece fresh root ginger, finely chopped

1 bunch spring onions, diagonally sliced

30ml/2 tbsp white vermouth

250ml/8fl oz/1 cup crème fraîche

salt and ground black pepper

chopped fresh parsley, to garnish

1 Place the butter in a shallow microwaveproof dish. Microwave on HIGH for 30 seconds to melt.

2 Remove the tough muscle opposite the red coral on each scallop. Separate the coral and cut the white part of the scallop in half horizontally. Add the scallops, including the corals, cover and microwave on HIGH for 4–6 minutes, rearranging once.

3 Lift out the scallops with a slotted spoon and transfer them to a warmed serving dish. Keep warm.

4 Add the ginger and spring onions to the juices in the bowl and microwave on HIGH for 1 minute. Pour in the vermouth and microwave on HIGH for 30 seconds. Stir in the crème fraîche and microwave on HIGH for 1–1½ minutes, stirring twice. Taste and adjust the seasoning.

5 Pour the sauce over the scallops, sprinkle with parsley and serve.

Eggs en Cocotte

A classic starter, these baked eggs are cooked on a flavoursome base of ratatouille, making them ideal for microwave cooking. They are also excellent for lunch or supper, with plenty of warm crusty bread.

INGREDIENTS

Serves 4

4 eggs

20ml/4 tsp freshly grated Parmesan cheese

chopped fresh parsley, to garnish

For the ratatouille

1 small red pepper

15ml/1 tbsp olive oil

1 onion, finely chopped

1 garlic clove, crushed

2 courgettes, diced

400g/14oz can chopped tomatoes
  with basil

salt and ground black pepper

1 First prepare the vegetables: cut the red pepper in half on a board and remove the seeds. Then dice the pepper flesh.

2 Place the oil in a microwave-proof bowl. Add the onion, garlic, courgettes and pepper, and microwave on HIGH for 3–4 minutes, stirring once, until softened. Stir in the tomatoes, with salt and pepper to taste, and microwave on HIGH for 3–4 minutes, stirring once.

3 Divide the ratatouille between four individual microwave-proof dishes or large ramekins, each with a capacity of about 300ml/½ pint/1¼ cups.

4 Make a small hollow in the centre of each portion of ratatouille and break in an egg.

5 Grind some black pepper over the top of each cocotte and sprinkle with the cheese. Gently prick each yolk with a needle or wooden cocktail stick. Microwave on HIGH for 4–6 minutes or until the eggs are just set. Sprinkle with the fresh parsley and serve at once.

Mushroom Pâté

This is a vegetarian alternative to liver-based pâtés. Cooking the onion in butter gives a rich flavour, but you can use oil instead, if preferred.

Serves 4

30ml/2 tbsp olive oil or butter

2 onions, chopped

350g/12oz/4½ cups mushrooms, chopped
   or roughly sliced

225g/8oz/1 cup ground almonds

a handful of parsley, stalks removed

salt and ground black pepper

flat leaf parsley, to garnish

thin slices of toast, cucumber, chicory and
   celery sticks, to serve

1 Place the olive oil or butter in a microwaveproof bowl with the onions. Microwave on HIGH for 5–7 minutes, stirring twice.

2 Add the mushrooms and microwave on HIGH for 3–3½ minutes, stirring halfway through cooking. Season well.

3 Transfer the cooked onion and mushrooms to a blender or food processor with their juices. Add the ground almonds and parsley, and process briefly. The pâté can either be smooth or you can leave it slightly chunky. Taste again for seasoning.

4 Spoon the pâté into individual pots. Garnish with flat leaf parsley and serve with thin slices of toast and sticks of cucumber, chicory and celery.

Stuffed Vine Leaves

Based on the Greek dolmas (or dolmades) but with a wholegrain vegetarian stuffing, this makes an excellent low-fat, high-fibre starter, snack or buffet dish. This is a quick version of the traditional speciality – the leaves and filling are cooked separately, rather than by long, slow cooking together for the authentic dish.

INGREDIENTS

Makes about 40

15ml/1 tbsp sunflower oil

5ml/1 tsp sesame oil

1 onion, finely chopped

225g/8oz/1⅓ cups brown rice

600ml/1 pint/2½ cups hot vegetable stock

1 small yellow pepper, seeded and finely chopped

115g/4oz/⅔ cup ready-to-eat dried apricots, finely chopped

2 lemons

50g/2oz/½ cup pine nuts

45ml/3 tbsp chopped fresh parsley

30ml/2 tbsp chopped fresh mint

2.5ml/½ tsp mixed spice

225g/8oz packet vine leaves preserved in brine, drained

150ml/¼ pint/⅔ cup water

30ml/2 tbsp olive oil

ground black pepper

lemon wedges, to garnish

To serve

300ml/½ pint/1¼ cups low-fat natural yogurt

30ml/2 tbsp chopped fresh mixed herbs

cayenne pepper

1 Place the sunflower and sesame oils together in a large microwaveproof bowl. Microwave on HIGH for 30 seconds. Add the onion and microwave on HIGH for 2 minutes, stirring once.

2 Add the rice and stir to coat the grains in oil. Pour in the stock, cover loosely and microwave on HIGH for 3 minutes. Reduce the power setting to MEDIUM and microwave for a further 25 minutes, stirring two or three times.

3 Stir in the chopped pepper and apricots. Replace the cover and leave to stand for 5 minutes.

4 Grate the rind off 1 lemon, then squeeze both lemons. Drain off any stock that has not been absorbed by the rice. Stir in the pine nuts, herbs, mixed spice, lemon rind and half the juice. Season with pepper and set aside.

5 Place the vine leaves in a bowl with the water, cover and microwave on HIGH for 4 minutes. Drain the leaves well, then lay them shiny side down on a board. Cut out any coarse stalks.

6 Place a heap of the rice mixture in the centre of a vine leaf. Fold over first the stem end, then the sides and finally the pointed end to make a neat parcel. Repeat with the remaining leaves.

7 Pack the parcels closely together in a shallow serving dish. Mix the remaining lemon juice with the olive oil and pour over the vine leaves. Cover and chill before serving.

8 Serve the vine leaves, garnished with lemon wedges. Spoon the yogurt into a bowl, stir in the chopped herbs and sprinkle with a little cayenne. Offer this light sauce with the chilled stuffed vine leaves.

COOK'S TIP

If vine leaves are not available, the leaves of Swiss chard, young spinach or cabbage can be used instead.

FISH AND SEAFOOD

Mediterranean Plaice

Sun-dried tomatoes, toasted pine nuts and anchovies make a flavoursome combination for the stuffing mixture.

INGREDIENTS

Serves 4

4 plaice fillets, about 225g/8oz each, skinned

75g/3oz/6 tbsp butter

1 small onion, chopped

1 celery stick, finely chopped

115g/4oz/2 cups fresh white breadcrumbs

45ml/3 tbsp chopped fresh parsley

30ml/2 tbsp pine nuts, toasted

3–4 pieces sun-dried tomatoes in oil, drained and chopped

50g/2oz can anchovy fillets, drained and chopped

75ml/5 tbsp fish stock

ground black pepper

1 Using a sharp knife, cut the plaice fillets in half lengthways to make eight smaller fillets.

2 Place the butter in a microwaveproof bowl and add the onion and celery. Cover and microwave on HIGH for 2 minutes, stirring halfway through cooking.

3 Mix together the bread-crumbs, parsley, pine nuts, sun-dried tomatoes and anchovies. Stir in the softened vegetables with their buttery juices and season with pepper.

4 Divide the stuffing into eight portions. Taking one portion at a time, form the stuffing into balls, then roll up each one inside a plaice fillet. Secure each roll with a wooden cocktail stick.

5 Place the rolled fillets in a buttered microwaveproof dish. Pour in the stock and cover the dish. Microwave on HIGH for 6–8 minutes, or until the fish flakes easily. Remove the cocktail sticks, then serve with a little of the cooking juices drizzled over.

Fisherman's Casserole

A perfect dish for microwaving as it's cooked in one dish.

INGREDIENTS

Serves 4–6

450g/1lb mixed firm fish fillets, such as
   cod, haddock and monkfish

50g/2oz/4 tbsp butter

1 onion, sliced

1 celery stick, sliced

350g/12oz potatoes, cut into chunks

750ml/1¼ pints/3 cups hot fish stock

bouquet garni

150g/5oz frozen broad beans

300ml/½ pint/1¼ cups milk

115g/4oz peeled cooked prawns

8 mussels, shelled

salt and ground black pepper

chopped parsley, to garnish

1 Skin the fish and cut the flesh into bite-sized chunks using a large sharp knife. Place the butter in a microwaveproof dish and microwave on HIGH for 1 minute, until melted. Add the onion, celery and potatoes, cover and microwave on HIGH for 4 minutes, stirring once during cooking.

2 Stir in the stock, bouquet garni and beans. Cover and microwave on HIGH for 10 minutes, stirring twice.

3 Add the fish and milk, re-cover and microwave on HIGH for 5–7 minutes until the fish flakes. Stir in the prawns, mussels and seasoning and microwave on HIGH for 1–2 minutes to warm through. Sprinkle with parsley and serve.

Potato-topped Fish Pie

Cheese-topped potatoes enclose a creamy mixture of fish, prawns and hard-boiled eggs.

INGREDIENTS

Serves 4

400ml/14fl oz/1⅔ cups hot milk

1 bay leaf

¼ onion, sliced

450g/1lb haddock or cod fillet

225g/8oz smoked haddock fillet

3 hard-boiled eggs, chopped

65g/2½oz/5 tbsp butter

25g/1oz/2 tbsp plain flour

115g/4oz/1 cup frozen peas

75g/3oz peeled cooked prawns

30ml/2 tbsp chopped fresh parsley

lemon juice, to taste

500g/1¼lb cooked potatoes, mashed

60ml/4 tbsp grated Cheddar cheese

salt and ground black pepper

1 Place 120ml/4fl oz/½ cup of the milk, the bay leaf and onion in a microwaveproof dish, then add the white and smoked fish. Cover and microwave on HIGH for 7–8 minutes, rearranging once. Strain and reserve the milk. Flake the fish into a microwaveproof pie dish, discarding the skin and any bones. Add the eggs.

2 Place 25g/1oz/2 tbsp of the butter, the flour and remaining milk in a microwaveproof jug. Whisk in the reserved cooking liquid from the fish. Microwave on HIGH for 5–7 minutes, stirring every 1 minute, until smooth, boiling and thickened. Stir in the peas and cooked prawns.

3 Add the parsley, lemon juice and seasoning to taste. Pour the sauce over the fish and eggs and carefully mix the ingredients.

4 Spoon the mashed potato evenly over the fish and fork up the surface. Dot with the remaining butter.

5 Sprinkle the cheese over the pie, then microwave on HIGH for 5–6 minutes. Brown under a preheated hot grill, if liked. Serve piping hot.

COMBINATION MICROWAVE

This recipe is suitable for cooking in a combination microwave. Follow your oven manufacturer's timing guide for good results.

Tuna and Mixed Vegetable Pasta

Cook this simple and very speedy sauce in the microwave while the pasta cooks conventionally.

INGREDIENTS

Serves 4

30ml/2 tbsp olive oil

175g/6oz/1½ cups button mushrooms, sliced

1 garlic clove, crushed

½ red pepper, seeded and chopped

15ml/1 tbsp tomato purée

300ml/½ pint/1¼ cups tomato juice

115g/4oz frozen peas

15–30ml/1–2 tbsp drained pickled green peppercorns, crushed

275g/10oz/2½ cups wholewheat pasta shapes

200g/7oz can tuna chunks in brine, drained

6 spring onions, diagonally sliced

1 Place the oil in a microwave-proof bowl with the mushrooms, garlic and pepper. Cover and microwave on HIGH for 4 minutes, stirring halfway through cooking. Stir in the tomato purée, then add the tomato juice, peas and some or all of the crushed peppercorns, depending on how spicy you like the sauce.

2 Cover the bowl and microwave on HIGH for a further 4 minutes, stirring halfway through cooking.

3 Bring a large saucepan of lightly salted water to the boil on the hob and cook the pasta for about 12 minutes, or according to the packet instructions, until just tender. When the pasta is almost ready, add the tuna to the sauce and microwave on HIGH for 1 minute to heat though. Stir in the spring onions. Drain the pasta and tip it into a warmed bowl. Pour the sauce over the pasta and toss to mix. Serve at once.

Sweet and Sour Fish

Serve this tasty, nutritious dish with brown rice and stir-fried cabbage or spinach for a delicious, light lunchtime meal.

INGREDIENTS

Serves 4

60ml/4 tbsp cider vinegar

45ml/3 tbsp light soy sauce

50g/2oz/¼ cup granulated sugar

15ml/1 tbsp tomato purée

25ml/1½ tbsp cornflour

250ml/8fl oz/1 cup water

1 green pepper, seeded and sliced

225g/8oz can pineapple pieces in fruit juice

225g/8oz tomatoes, peeled and chopped

225g/8oz/2 cups button mushrooms, sliced

675g/1½lb chunky haddock fillets, skinned

salt and ground black pepper

1 Mix the vinegar, soy sauce, sugar and tomato purée in a microwaveproof bowl. Gradually blend the cornflour to a smooth paste with the water, then add to the bowl, stirring well. Microwave on HIGH for 2–2½ minutes, stirring three times during cooking, until smooth, boiling and thickened.

2 Add the green pepper, canned pineapple pieces (with juice), tomatoes and mushrooms to the sauce and microwave on HIGH for 2 minutes, stirring halfway through cooking. Season to taste with salt and pepper.

3 Place the fish in a single layer in a shallow microwaveproof dish and pour over the sauce. Cover and microwave on HIGH for 8–10 minutes, rotating the dish twice during cooking. Leave to stand for 5 minutes before serving.

Green Fish Curry

Serves 4

1.5ml/¼ tsp ground turmeric

30ml/2 tbsp lime juice

pinch of salt

4 portions cod fillets, skinned and cut into
   5cm/2in chunks

1 onion, chopped

1 green chilli, roughly chopped

1 garlic clove, crushed

25g/1oz/¼ cup cashew nuts

2.5ml/½ tsp fennel seeds

30ml/2 tbsp desiccated coconut

30ml/2 tbsp oil

1.5ml/¼ tsp cumin seeds

1.5ml/¼ tsp ground coriander

1.5ml/¼ tsp ground cumin

1.5ml/¼ tsp salt

150ml/¼ pint/⅔ cup water

175ml/6fl oz/¾ cup single cream

45ml/3 tbsp finely chopped fresh
   coriander

fresh coriander sprig, to garnish

rice with vegetables, to serve

1 Mix the turmeric, lime juice and pinch of salt, then rub the mixture over the fish. Cover and leave to marinate for 15 minutes.

2 Meanwhile, process the onion, chilli, garlic, cashew nuts, fennel seeds and coconut to a paste in a blender or food processor. Spoon the paste into a bowl and set it aside.

3 Place the oil in a large microwaveproof bowl. Add the cumin seeds and microwave on HIGH for 1–1½ minutes or until the seeds begin to splutter. Add the paste, ground coriander, cumin, salt and water and mix well. Cover and microwave on HIGH for 3–5 minutes, stirring twice during cooking.

4 Stir in the cream and fresh coriander. Microwave on HIGH for a further 2–3 minutes, stirring halfway through cooking.

5 Gently mix in the fish. Cover and microwave on HIGH for 7–10 minutes, stirring twice, until cooked. Serve, garnished with coriander, with rice and vegetables or pilau.

COOK'S TIP

Whole and ground spices, lime, garlic, chilli and coconut make a superb sauce. Fresh coriander and single cream balance and enliven the flavours.

Prawn Curry

This rich prawn curry is flavoured with coconut and a delicious blend of aromatic spices.

INGREDIENTS

Serves 4

675g/1½lb uncooked tiger prawns

4 dried red chillies

50g/2oz/1 cup desiccated coconut

5ml/1 tsp black mustard seeds

1 large onion, chopped

45ml/3 tbsp oil

4 bay leaves

2.5cm/1in piece fresh root ginger, finely
  chopped

2 garlic cloves, crushed

15ml/1 tbsp ground coriander

5ml/1 tsp chilli powder

5ml/1 tsp salt

4 tomatoes, finely chopped

175ml/6fl oz/¾ cup water

plain rice, to serve

1 Peel the prawns. Run a sharp knife along the back of each prawn to make a shallow cut and carefully remove the thin black intestinal vein.

2 Put the dried red chillies, coconut, mustard seeds and onion in a large microwaveproof bowl. Microwave on HIGH for 8 minutes, stirring twice. Process the mixture to a coarse paste in a blender or food processor.

3 Place the oil in a microwave-proof bowl with the bay leaves. Add the ginger and garlic, cover and microwave on HIGH for 2 minutes, stirring twice during cooking.

4 Stir in the coriander, chilli powder, salt and the paste. Cover and microwave on HIGH for 2–3 minutes, stirring halfway through cooking.

5 Stir in the tomatoes and water, cover and microwave on HIGH for 4–6 minutes, stirring halfway through cooking, until thickened slightly.

6 Mix in the prawns, cover and microwave on HIGH for 4 minutes or until they turn pink and their edges curl slightly. Serve with plain boiled rice.

Seafood Pilaff

This all-in-one main course makes a satisfying meal for any day of the week. For a special meal, substitute dry white wine for the orange juice.

INGREDIENTS

Serves 4

10ml/2 tsp olive oil

250g/9oz/1¼ cups long grain rice

5ml/1 tsp ground turmeric

1 red pepper, seeded and diced

1 small onion, finely chopped

2 courgettes, sliced

150g/5oz/2 cups button mushrooms, halved

350ml/12fl oz/1½ cups fish or chicken stock

150ml/¼ pint/⅔ cup orange juice

350g/12oz white fish fillets, skinned

12 cooked mussels, shelled

salt and ground black pepper

grated rind of 1 orange, to garnish

1 Mix the oil with the rice and turmeric in a large microwaveproof bowl. Microwave on HIGH for 1 minute.

2 Add the pepper, onion, courgettes and mushrooms. Stir in the stock and orange juice. Cover and microwave on HIGH for 13 minutes, stirring halfway through cooking. Leave to stand, covered.

3 Place the fish on a microwaveproof plate. Cover and microwave on HIGH for 4–5 minutes, until cooked. Flake the fish and stir it into the rice mixture. Stir in the mussels and microwave on HIGH for a further 1 minute. Adjust the seasoning, sprinkle with orange rind and serve hot.

Salmon Pasta with Parsley Sauce

INGREDIENTS

Serves 4

450g/1lb salmon fillet, skinned

225g/8oz/3 cups pasta shapes, such as penne or twists

175g/6oz cherry tomatoes, halved

150ml/¼ pint/⅔ cup low-fat crème fraîche

45ml/3 tbsp chopped fresh parsley

finely grated rind of ½ orange

salt and ground black pepper

COOK'S TIP

If low-fat crème fraîche is not available, use ordinary crème fraîche or double cream instead.

1 Cut the salmon into bite-sized pieces, arrange them on a microwaveproof plate and cover with greaseproof paper. Microwave on HIGH for 2–2½ minutes, rearranging halfway through cooking. Leave to stand for 5 minutes.

2 Cook the pasta in a saucepan of boiling water on the hob, following the packet instructions.

3 Alternatively, cook the pasta in 1.2 litres/2 pints boiling water with 5ml/1 tsp oil in a large microwaveproof bowl. Microwave on HIGH for 10–12 minutes.

4 Drain the pasta and toss it with the tomatoes and salmon. Mix the crème fraîche, parsley, orange rind and pepper to taste, then toss this sauce into the salmon and pasta and serve hot.

Whole Cooked Salmon

Farmed salmon has made this fish more affordable and less of a treat, but a whole salmon still features as a centrepiece at parties. As with all fish, the taste depends first on freshness and second on not overcooking it. Although you need to start early, the cooking time is short. Cooked salmon is, of course, also delicious served hot with a buttery hollandaise sauce. New potatoes and fine green beans are perfect accompaniments.

INGREDIENTS

Serves 6–8 as part of a buffet

1.8kg/4lb whole salmon

1 lemon, sliced

salt and ground black pepper

lemon wedges, cucumber ribbons and
    fresh dill sprigs, to garnish

1 Wash the salmon and dry it well, inside and out. Prick the skin in several places to prevent bursting and place the salmon in a shallow microwaveproof dish.

2 Put a few slices of lemon inside the salmon and arrange some more on the top. Season well and sprinkle a little boiling water over to moisten the fish.

3 Cover with greaseproof paper or vented clear film and microwave on HIGH for 20–22 minutes, rotating the dish three times during cooking. Leave to stand, covered, for 5 minutes, before serving hot. If serving cold, leave to cool completely before uncovering.

4 To serve hot with hollandaise sauce, peel away the skin and transfer the salmon to a heated serving dish. Keep warm while preparing the sauce.

5 To serve cold and on the same day, remove the skin from the cooked fish and arrange it on a large platter. Garnish with lemon wedges, cucumber cut into thin ribbons and sprigs of dill. If you intend serving the salmon the following day, leave the skin on and chill the fish overnight before adding the garnish.

HOLLANDAISE SAUCE

Place 115g/4oz/8 tbsp butter in a large microwaveproof jug and microwave on HIGH for 1½ minutes. Whisk in 45ml/3 tbsp lemon juice, 2 egg yolks, a pinch of mustard powder and salt and pepper to taste. Microwave on MEDIUM for 1 minute, then whisk and serve.

COOK'S TIP

To prevent the head and tail ends of fish from overcooking in the microwave, they can be shielded with small pieces of smooth foil. This may be done at the beginning of the cooking time or after a few minutes if cooking progress is being carefully watched.

MEAT AND
POULTRY

~

Lamb Pie with a Potato Crust

INGREDIENTS

Serves 4

675g/1½lb potatoes, diced

45ml/3 tbsp water

30ml/2 tbsp skimmed milk

15ml/1 tbsp wholegrain or
    French mustard

1 onion, chopped

2 celery sticks, sliced

2 carrots, diced

450g/1lb lean minced lamb

150ml/¼ pint/⅔ cup beef stock

60ml/4 tbsp rolled oats

15ml/1 tbsp Worcestershire sauce

30ml/2 tbsp chopped fresh rosemary

salt and ground black pepper

1 Place the potatoes in a microwaveproof bowl with the water. Cover and microwave on HIGH for 8–10 minutes, until tender, stirring once. Drain and mash until smooth, then stir in the milk and mustard.

2 Place the onion, celery and carrots in a large microwave-proof bowl. Cover and microwave on HIGH for 5 minutes, stirring once. Add the minced lamb, mixing well. Microwave on HIGH for 2 minutes, stirring once.

3 Stir in the stock, rolled oats, Worcestershire sauce and rosemary, and season to taste with salt and pepper. Cover loosely and microwave on HIGH for 20–25 minutes, until cooked, stirring twice.

4 Turn the meat mixture into a 1.75 litre/3 pint/7½ cup microwaveproof dish that is suitable for grilling. Swirl the potato evenly over the top. Microwave, uncovered, on HIGH for 4–5 minutes until hot. Brown under a grill, if liked. Serve with freshly cooked vegetables.

COMBINATION MICROWAVE

This recipe is suitable for cooking in a combination microwave. Follow the oven manufacturer's timing guide for good results.

Beef and Mushroom Burgers

It's worth making your own burgers to cut down on fat – in these, the meat is extended with mushrooms for extra fibre.

Serves 4

1 small onion, chopped

150g/5oz/2 cups small cup mushrooms

450g/1lb lean minced beef

50g/2oz/1 cup fresh wholemeal
   breadcrumbs

5ml/1 tsp dried mixed herbs

15ml/1 tbsp tomato purée

plain flour, for shaping

salt and ground black pepper

relish, lettuce, burger buns or pitta bread,
   to serve

1 Place the onion and mushrooms in a food processor and process until finely chopped. Add the beef, breadcrumbs, herbs, tomato purée and seasoning. Process for a few seconds, until the mixture binds together but still has some texture.

2 Divide the mixture into four, then press into burger shapes using lightly floured hands.

3 To cook, place the burgers on a microwaveproof roasting rack and microwave, uncovered, for 6–7 minutes, turning over once. Leave to stand for 2–3 minutes.

4 Alternatively, for a browner and crisper result, preheat a microwave browning dish according to the manufacturer's instructions. Add the burgers, pressing down well on to the base and microwave on HIGH for 5–5½ minutes, turning over once. Leave to stand for 2–3 minutes. Serve with relish and lettuce, in burger buns or pitta bread.

VARIATION

To make Lamb and Mushroom Burgers, substitute lean minced lamb for the minced beef.

COMBINATION MICROWAVE

This recipe is suitable for cooking in a combination microwave. Follow the oven manufacturer's timing guide for good results.

Stuffed Tomatoes

Ever popular, this simple recipe demonstrates the versatility of mince as a stuffing.

INGREDIENTS

Serves 4

4 beef tomatoes

7.5ml/1½ tsp oil

75g/3oz/¾ cup minced beef

1 small red onion, thinly sliced

25g/1oz/¼ cup bulgur wheat

30ml/2 tbsp freshly grated
   Parmesan cheese

15g/½oz/1 tbsp cashew nuts, chopped

1 small celery stick, chopped

salt and ground black pepper

crisp green salad, to serve

1 Trim the tops from the tomatoes, scoop out the flesh with a teaspoon and reserve.

2 Place the oil in a large microwaveproof bowl, add the minced beef and onion, cover and microwave on HIGH for 5–6 minutes or until the beef is cooked, stirring twice to break up the meat. Stir in the tomato flesh.

3 Place the bulgur wheat in a bowl, cover with boiling water and leave to soak for 10 minutes. Drain if necessary.

4 Mix the mince and bulgur, Parmesan cheese, nuts and celery. Season well.

5 Spoon the filling into the tomatoes and place in a shallow microwaveproof dish. Microwave on HIGH for 3–5 minutes or until the tomatoes and their filling are tender. Serve with a crisp green salad.

Spicy Bolognese

A spicy version of a popular dish. Worcestershire sauce and chorizo sausages add an extra element to this perfect family standby.

INGREDIENTS

Serves 4

15ml/1 tbsp oil
1 onion, chopped
225g/8oz/2 cups minced beef
5ml/1 tsp ground chilli powder
15ml/1 tbsp Worcestershire sauce
25g/1oz/2 tbsp plain flour
150ml/¼ pint/⅔ cup beef stock
4 chorizo sausages
200g/7oz can chopped tomatoes
50g/2oz baby sweetcorn
15ml/1 tbsp chopped fresh basil
salt and ground black pepper

1 Place the oil and onion in a large microwaveproof bowl. Microwave on HIGH for 2 minutes. Add the minced beef and chilli powder, mixing well. Microwave on HIGH for 4–5 minutes, breaking up the mince twice during cooking.

2 Stir in the Worcestershire sauce and flour. Microwave on HIGH for 30 seconds, stirring once, before pouring in the stock.

3 Slice the chorizo sausages and halve the corn lengthways.

4 Stir in the sausages, tomatoes, sweetcorn and chopped basil. Season well, cover loosely and microwave on HIGH for 15–20 minutes, stirring twice. Serve with spaghetti, garnished with fresh basil.

COOK'S TIP

If you like, cool the Bolognese sauce and freeze it in conveniently sized portions for up to 2 months.

Hot Chilli Chicken

Not for the faint-hearted, this fiery, hot curry is made with a spicy chilli masala paste.

INGREDIENTS

Serves 4

30ml/2 tbsp tomato purée
2 garlic cloves, roughly chopped
2 green chillies, roughly chopped
5 dried red chillies
2.5ml/½ tsp salt
1.5ml/¼ tsp sugar
5ml/1 tsp chilli powder
2.5ml/½ tsp paprika
15ml/1 tbsp curry paste
30ml/2 tbsp oil
2.5ml/½ tsp cumin seeds
1 onion, finely chopped
2 bay leaves
5ml/1 tsp ground coriander
5ml/1 tsp ground cumin
1.5ml/¼ tsp ground turmeric
400g/14oz can chopped tomatoes
150ml/¼ pint/⅔ cup water
8 chicken thighs, skinned
5ml/1 tsp garam masala
sliced green chillies, to garnish
chappatis and natural yogurt, to serve

1 Process the tomato purée, garlic, green and dried red chillies, salt, sugar, chilli powder, paprika and curry paste to a smooth paste in a food processor or blender.

2 Place the oil in a large microwaveproof bowl and add the cumin seeds. Microwave on HIGH for 1½ minutes. Add the onion and bay leaves, cover and microwave on HIGH for 3 minutes.

3 Stir in the chilli paste. Cover and microwave on HIGH for 1½ minutes, then mix in the remaining ground spices, chopped tomatoes and water. Cover and microwave on HIGH for 3 minutes.

4 Add the chicken and garam masala. Cover and microwave on HIGH for 18–22 minutes, stirring twice, until the chicken is tender. Garnish with sliced green chillies and serve with chappatis and natural yogurt.

Chicken and Fruit Salad

The chicken may be cooked a day before serving and the salad assembled at the last minute. Serve with warm garlic bread.

INGREDIENTS

Serves 8

4 tarragon or rosemary sprigs

2 x 1.5kg/3–3½lb chickens

65g/2½oz/5 tbsp softened butter

150ml/¼ pint/⅔ cup chicken stock

150ml/¼ pint/⅔ cup white wine

1 small cantaloupe melon

115g/4oz/1 cup walnut pieces

lettuce leaves

450g/1lb seedless grapes or
    cherries, stoned

salt and ground black pepper

For the dressing

30ml/2 tbsp tarragon vinegar

120ml/8 tbsp light olive oil

30ml/2 tbsp chopped mixed fresh herbs,
    for example parsley, mint and tarragon

1 Put the sprigs of tarragon or rosemary inside the chickens and season with salt and pepper. Tie the chickens in a neat shape with string and spread with 50g/2oz/4 tbsp of the softened butter. Place breast-side down in a microwaveproof shallow dish and pour round the stock. Cover loosely and microwave on HIGH for 30–35 minutes, turning breast-side up halfway through cooking. Cover with foil and leave to stand for 10–15 minutes. Prick to release excess juices and leave to cool.

2 Add the wine to the cooking juices. Transfer to a microwaveproof jug or bowl and microwave on HIGH for about 5 minutes or until syrupy. Strain and leave the juices to cool. Scoop the melon into balls or into cubes. Joint the chickens.

3 Place the remaining butter in a microwaveproof bowl with the walnuts. Microwave on HIGH for 2–3 minutes to brown, stirring once. Drain and cool.

4 To make the dressing, whisk the vinegar and oil together with some seasoning. Remove the fat from the chicken juices and add the juices to the dressing with the herbs. Adjust the seasoning.

5 Arrange the chicken pieces on a bed of lettuce, scatter over the grapes or stoned cherries, melon balls or cubes and coat with the herb dressing. Sprinkle with toasted walnuts and serve.

COMBINATION MICROWAVE

This recipe is suitable for cooking in a combination microwave. Follow the oven manufacturer's timing guide for good results.

COOK'S TIP

The chickens can be cooked in roasting bags, but do not use metal ties for securing the bags; replace with elastic bands or string.

Chicken Liver Salad

This salad may be served as a first course on individual plates.

INGREDIENTS

Serves 4

mixed salad leaves, such as frisée and
    oakleaf lettuce or radicchio
1 avocado, diced
2 pink grapefruits, segmented
350g/12oz chicken livers
30ml/2 tbsp olive oil
1 garlic clove, crushed
salt and ground black pepper
crusty bread, to serve

For the dressing
30ml/2 tbsp lemon juice
60ml/4 tbsp olive oil
2.5ml/½ tsp wholegrain mustard
2.5ml/½ tsp clear honey
15ml/1 tbsp snipped fresh chives

1 First prepare the dressing: put all the ingredients into a screw-topped jar and shake vigorously to emulsify the mixture. Taste and adjust the seasoning.

2 Wash and dry the salad. Arrange attractively on a serving plate with the avocado and grapefruit.

3 Dry the chicken livers on paper towels and remove any sinew or membrane. Cut the larger livers in half and leave the smaller ones whole. Prick thoroughly with a fork.

4 Place the oil in a large microwaveproof bowl. Add the livers and garlic, mixing well. Cover loosely and microwave on HIGH for 3–4 minutes, stirring twice until cooked, but still slightly pink inside.

5 Season with salt and ground black pepper and drain on paper towels.

6 Place the liver on the salad and spoon the dressing over the top. Serve immediately, with warm crusty bread.

PULSES, PASTA
AND GRAINS

Borlotti Beans with Mushrooms

A mixture of wild and cultivated mushrooms helps to give this dish a rich and nutty flavour.

INGREDIENTS

Serves 4

30ml/2 tbsp olive oil

50g/2oz/4 tbsp butter

2 shallots, chopped

2-3 garlic cloves, crushed

675g/1½lb mixed mushrooms,
   thickly sliced

4 sun-dried tomatoes in oil, drained
   and chopped

45ml/3 tbsp dry white wine

400g/14oz can borlotti beans

45ml/3 tbsp grated Parmesan cheese

30ml/2 tbsp chopped fresh parsley

salt and ground black pepper

freshly cooked pappardelle pasta, to serve

1 Place the oil and butter in a microwaveproof bowl with the shallots. Microwave on HIGH for 1 minute.

2 Add the garlic and mushrooms and microwave on HIGH for 3–4 minutes, stirring halfway through cooking. Stir in the sun-dried tomatoes, wine and seasoning to taste.

3 Stir in the borlotti beans and microwave on HIGH for 2–3 minutes or until the beans are heated through.

4 Stir in the grated Parmesan and sprinkle with parsley. Serve immediately with hot pappardelle pasta.

COOK'S TIP

When buying wild mushrooms, examine packs carefully and reject any mushrooms that have tiny holes or show signs of being eaten as they may contain tiny maggots.

Pasta Carbonara

Cooking the pasta conventionally on the hob and the sauce in the microwave makes this a very speedy dish to prepare.

INGREDIENTS

Serves 4

350–450g/12oz–1lb fresh tagliatelle

15ml/1 tbsp olive oil

225g/8oz ham, bacon or pancetta, cut into
   2.5cm/1in sticks

115g/4oz button mushrooms
   (about 10), sliced

4 eggs, lightly beaten

75ml/5 tbsp single cream

30ml/2 tbsp finely grated
   Parmesan cheese

salt and ground black pepper

fresh basil sprigs, to garnish

1 While preparing the sauce in the microwave, cook the pasta conventionally in a large saucepan of boiling salted water on the hob according to the packet instructions.

2 Meanwhile, place the oil and ham in a microwaveproof bowl. Microwave on HIGH for 3 minutes, then add the mushrooms. Microwave on HIGH for a further 3 minutes, stirring once during cooking. Meanwhile, lightly beat the eggs and cream together and season well.

3 Drain the cooked pasta well and add to the ham and mushroom mixture, mixing well.

4 Pour in the eggs and cream and add half the Parmesan cheese. Stir well and, as you do this, the eggs will cook in the heat of the pasta. If you like your sauce slightly thicker, then microwave on HIGH for 30 seconds, stirring once during cooking. Pile on to warmed serving plates, sprinkle with the remaining Parmesan and garnish with basil.

Baked Macaroni Cheese

A delicious supper-time dish – replace the Cheddar with your family's favourite cheese.

INGREDIENTS

Serves 4

275g/10oz/2⅓ cups macaroni

1.2 litres/2 pints/5 cups boiling water

15ml/1 tbsp olive oil

2 leeks, chopped

50g/2oz/4 tbsp butter

50g/2oz/½ cup plain flour

900ml/1½ pints/3¾ cups milk

225g/8oz/2 cups mature Cheddar
   cheese, grated

30ml/2 tbsp fromage frais

5ml/1 tsp wholegrain mustard

50g/2oz/1 cup fresh white breadcrumbs

25g/1oz/½ cup Double Gloucester
   cheese, grated

salt and ground black pepper

15ml/1 tbsp chopped fresh parsley,
   to garnish

1 Place the macaroni in a large microwaveproof bowl with the boiling water and the olive oil. Add the leeks and microwave on HIGH for 10 minutes, stirring once. Leave to stand, covered, while cooking the sauce.

2 Stir the butter with the flour and milk in a large microwaveproof jug. Microwave on HIGH for 6–8 minutes, whisking every minute, until smooth, boiling and thickened.

3 Whisk in the Cheddar cheese, fromage frais and mustard, adding salt and pepper to taste.

4 Drain the macaroni and leeks and rinse under cold water. Stir the drained macaroni and leeks into the cheese sauce and turn into a dish that is suitable for grilling. Level the top with the back of a spoon and sprinkle over the breadcrumbs and Double Gloucester cheese.

5 Cook under a preheated hot grill until golden and bubbly. Serve hot, garnished with chopped fresh parsley.

Rigatoni with Spicy Sausage and Tomato

This is really a cheat's Bolognese sauce using the wonderful fresh spicy sausages sold in every Italian delicatessen.

INGREDIENTS

Serves 4

450g/1lb fresh spicy Italian sausage

30ml/2 tbsp olive oil

1 onion, chopped

475ml/16fl oz/2 cups passata (smooth, thick, sieved tomatoes)

150ml/¼ pint/⅔ cup dry red wine

6 sun-dried tomatoes in oil, drained

450g/1lb/4 cups rigatoni or similar pasta

salt and ground black pepper

freshly grated Parmesan cheese, to serve

1 Squeeze the sausagemeat out of the skins into a bowl and break it up.

2 While preparing the sauce, cook the pasta conventionally in a saucepan of boiling salted water on the hob according to the packet instructions.

3 Place the oil in a microwave-proof bowl and add the onion. Microwave on HIGH for 3 minutes. Stir in the sausagemeat and microwave on HIGH for 5 minutes, stirring every minute to break up the meat. Stir in the passata and wine. Cover and microwave on HIGH for 4 minutes, stirring once.

4 Slice the sun-dried tomatoes and add them to the sauce. Microwave, uncovered, for 2 minutes, stirring once, then season to taste.

5 Drain the pasta well and top with the sauce. Serve with grated Parmesan cheese.

COOK'S TIP

If you cannot find fresh Italian sausage, season pork sausage-meat with a crushed garlic clove, a little dried oregano, grated nutmeg and a pinch of paprika. Mix well.

Golden Vegetable Paella

Serves 4

pinch of saffron strands or 5ml/1 tsp
  ground turmeric
750ml/1¼ pints/3 cups boiling vegetable
  or spicy stock
90ml/6 tbsp olive oil
2 large onions, sliced
3 garlic cloves, chopped
275g/10oz/1⅓ cups long grain rice
50g/2oz/⅓ cup wild rice
175g/6oz pumpkin or butternut
  squash, chopped
175g/6oz carrots, cut into
  matchstick strips
1 yellow pepper, seeded and sliced
4 tomatoes, peeled and chopped
115g/4oz oyster mushrooms, quartered
salt and ground black pepper
strips of red, yellow and green pepper,
  to garnish

1 If using saffron, place it in a small bowl with 45–60ml/ 3–4 tbsp of the stock. Leave to stand for 5 minutes. Meanwhile, place the oil in a large microwave-proof bowl with the onions and garlic, then microwave on HIGH for 4–4½ minutes, stirring once.

2 Stir both types of rice into the onion mixture and toss until coated in oil. Add the remaining stock, with the pumpkin or squash, and the saffron strands and liquid or turmeric.

3 Cover and microwave on HIGH for 3 minutes. Add the carrots, pepper, tomatoes, salt and black pepper. Cover again and microwave on HIGH for 2 minutes. Reduce the power setting to MEDIUM and microwave for a further 12 minutes, stirring twice, or until the rice is almost tender.

4 Finally, add the oyster mushrooms, check the seasoning, cover and microwave on HIGH for 1 minute. Leave to stand for 10 minutes, fluff up the rice with a fork, top with the peppers and serve.

Ravioli with Four Cheese Sauce

This is a smooth cheese sauce that coats the pasta very evenly.

INGREDIENTS

Serves 4

350g/12oz ravioli

1.75 litres/3 pints/7½ cups boiling water

50g/2oz/¼ cup butter

50g/2oz/¼ cup plain flour

475ml/16fl oz/2 cups milk

50g/2oz Parmesan cheese

50g/2oz Edam cheese

50g/2oz Gruyère cheese

50g/2oz fontina cheese

salt and ground black pepper

chopped fresh parsley, to garnish

1 Place the ravioli in a large microwaveproof bowl and pour in the boiling water. Microwave on HIGH for 10 minutes, stirring halfway through cooking. Leave to stand for 3 minutes.

2 Whisk the butter, flour and milk together in a microwave-proof jug. Microwave on HIGH for 5–7 minutes, whisking every minute, until smooth, boiling and thickened.

3 Grate the cheeses and stir them into the sauce until they are just beginning to melt. Add seasoning to taste.

4 Drain the pasta thoroughly and turn it into a large serving bowl. Pour over the sauce and toss to coat. Serve immediately, garnished with chopped parsley.

COOK'S TIP

If you cannot find all of the recommended cheeses, simply substitute your favourite types. Strong-flavoured hard cheeses are best for this type of sauce.

Mushroom, Leek and Cashew Nut Risotto

INGREDIENTS

Serves 4

225g/8oz/1⅓ cups brown rice

900ml/1½ pints/3 cups boiling vegetable
    stock or a mixture of boiling stock and
    dry white wine in the ratio 5:1

15ml/1 tbsp walnut or hazelnut oil

2 leeks, sliced

225g/8oz/2 cups mixed wild or cultivated
    mushrooms, trimmed and sliced

50g/2oz/½ cup cashew nuts

grated rind of 1 lemon

30ml/2 tbsp chopped fresh thyme

25g/1oz/scant ¼ cup pumpkin seeds

salt and ground black pepper

fresh thyme sprigs and lemon wedges,
    to garnish

1 Place the rice in a large microwaveproof bowl with the boiling stock (or stock and wine). Cover loosely and microwave on HIGH for 3 minutes. Reduce the power setting to MEDIUM and microwave for a further 25 minutes, stirring twice. Leave to stand, covered, while cooking the vegetable and nut mixture.

2 Place the oil in a large microwaveproof bowl with the leeks and mushrooms. Cover and microwave on HIGH for 3–4 minutes, stirring once.

3 Add the cashew nuts, grated lemon rind and chopped fresh thyme to the leeks and mushrooms and microwave on HIGH for 1 minute. Season to taste with salt and freshly ground black pepper.

4 Drain off any excess stock from the cooked rice and stir in the vegetable mixture. Turn the risotto into a serving dish. Scatter the pumpkin seeds over the top and garnish with the fresh thyme sprigs and lemon wedges. Serve the risotto at once.

Spiced Lentils and Rice

Lentils are cooked with whole and ground spices, potatoes, rice and onions to produce an authentic Indian-style risotto.

INGREDIENTS

Serves 4

150g/5oz/³⁄₄ cup toovar dhal or split
    red lentils
115g/4oz basmati rice
1 large potato
1 large onion
30ml/2 tbsp sunflower oil
4 whole cloves
1.5ml/¼ tsp cumin seeds
1.5ml/¼ tsp ground turmeric
10ml/2 tsp salt
300ml/½ pint/1¼ cups boiling water

1 Wash the toovar dhal or lentils and rice in several changes of cold water. Then leave to soak in plenty of cold water for 15 minutes. Drain well.

2 Peel the potato and cut it into 2.5cm/1in chunks.

3 Thinly slice the onion and set it aside until the whole spices are lightly cooked.

4 Place the sunflower oil in a large microwaveproof bowl with the cloves and cumin seeds. Microwave on HIGH for 2 minutes.

5 Add the onion and potatoes, cover and microwave on HIGH for 4 minutes, stirring once. Stir in the lentils and rice, turmeric, salt and water.

6 Cover and microwave on HIGH for 3 minutes. Reduce the power setting to MEDIUM and microwave for a further 12 minutes, stirring twice. Leave to stand, covered, for about 10 minutes before serving.

Sweet Vegetable Couscous

A wonderful combination of sweet vegetables and spices, this makes a substantial winter dish.

INGREDIENTS

Serves 4-6

1 generous pinch of saffron threads

45ml/3 tbsp boiling water

15ml/1 tbsp olive oil

1 red onion, sliced

2 garlic cloves, crushed

1-2 fresh red chillies, seeded and
   finely chopped

2.5ml/$\frac{1}{2}$ tsp ground ginger

2.5ml/$\frac{1}{2}$ tsp ground cinnamon

400g/14oz can chopped tomatoes

300ml/$\frac{1}{2}$ pint/1$\frac{1}{4}$ cups hot vegetable stock
   or water

4 carrots, peeled and cut into
   5mm/$\frac{1}{4}$in slices

2 turnips, peeled and cut into
   2cm/$\frac{3}{4}$in cubes

450g/1lb sweet potatoes, peeled and cut
   into 2cm/$\frac{3}{4}$in cubes

75g/3oz/$\frac{1}{3}$ cup raisins

2 courgettes, cut into 5mm/$\frac{1}{4}$in slices

400g/14oz can chick-peas, drained
   and rinsed

45ml/3 tbsp chopped fresh parsley

45ml/3 tbsp chopped fresh
   coriander leaves

450g/1lb quick-cook couscous

1 Sprinkle the saffron into the boiling water and set this aside to infuse.

2 Place the oil in a large microwaveproof bowl. Add the onion, garlic and chillies. Microwave on HIGH for 2 minutes, stirring halfway through cooking.

3 Add the ground ginger and cinnamon and microwave on HIGH for 1 minute.

4 Stir in the tomatoes, stock or water, infused saffron and liquid, carrots, turnips, sweet potatoes and raisins. Cover and microwave on HIGH for 15 minutes, stirring twice during cooking.

5 Add the courgettes, chick-peas, parsley and coriander, cover and microwave on HIGH for 5–8 minutes, stirring once, until the vegetables are tender.

6 Meanwhile, prepare the couscous following the packet instructions and serve it with the vegetables.

VEGETABLES
AND SALADS

Mixed Mushroom Ragout

*These mushrooms are delicious
served hot or cold and can be made
up to two days in advance.*

INGREDIENTS

Serves 4

1 small onion, finely chopped
1 garlic clove, crushed
5ml/1 tsp coriander seeds, crushed
30ml/2 tbsp red wine vinegar
15ml/1 tbsp soy sauce
15ml/1 tbsp dry sherry
10ml/2 tsp tomato purée
10ml/2 tsp soft light brown sugar
75ml/5 tbsp hot vegetable stock
115g/4oz baby button mushrooms
115g/4oz chestnut mushrooms, quartered
115g/4oz oyster mushrooms, sliced
salt and ground black pepper
sprig of fresh coriander, to garnish

1 Mix the onion, garlic, coriander
seeds, red wine vinegar, soy
sauce, sherry, tomato purée, sugar
and stock in a large microwaveproof
bowl. Cover and microwave on
HIGH for 3 minutes, stirring once.
Uncover and microwave on HIGH
for a further 2–3 minutes, or until
the liquid has reduced by half.

2 Add the mushrooms, mixing
well. Cover and microwave on
HIGH for 3–4 minutes, stirring
once, until tender.

3 Remove the mushrooms with
a slotted spoon and transfer
them to a warmed serving dish.

4 Microwave the juices on
HIGH for about 3–5 minutes,
or until reduced to about
75ml/5 tbsp. Season to taste with
salt and ground black pepper.

COOK'S TIP
~

If coriander is a favourite spice
of yours, then it is worth buying
a pepper mill and filling it with
coriander seeds. This way, you
can grind a little coriander into
all sorts of savoury dishes to add
a hint of exotic seasoning.

5 Allow to cool for 2–3 minutes,
then pour over the
mushrooms. Serve hot or well
chilled, garnished with a sprig of
fresh coriander.

Spring Vegetable Medley

A colourful, dazzling medley of fresh and sweet young vegetables.

Serves 4

15ml/1 tbsp peanut oil

1 garlic clove, sliced

2.5cm/1in piece fresh ginger root, finely chopped

115g/4oz baby carrots

115g/4oz patty pan squash

115g/4oz baby sweetcorn

115g/4oz French beans, topped and tailed

115g/4oz sugar snap peas, topped and tailed

115g/4oz young asparagus, cut into 7.5cm/3in pieces

8 spring onions, trimmed and cut into 5cm/2in pieces

115g/4oz cherry tomatoes

For the dressing

juice of 2 limes

15ml/1 tbsp runny honey

15ml/1 tbsp soy sauce

5ml/1 tsp sesame oil

1 Place the peanut oil in a large microwaveproof bowl.

2 Add the garlic and ginger, and microwave on HIGH for 30 seconds.

3 Stir in the carrots, patty pan squash, sweetcorn and beans. Cover and microwave on HIGH for 5 minutes, stirring halfway through cooking.

4 Add the sugar snap peas, asparagus, spring onions and cherry tomatoes. Cover and microwave on HIGH for 3–4 minutes, stirring halfway through cooking.

5 Mix the dressing ingredients together and add to the bowl.

6 Stir well, then cover again and microwave on HIGH for 1–2 minutes, or until the vegetables are just tender but still crisp.

Middle-Eastern Vegetable Stew

A spiced dish of mixed vegetables makes a delicious and filling vegetarian main course. Children may prefer less chilli.

INGREDIENTS

Serves 4-6

45ml/3 tbsp vegetable stock

1 green pepper, seeded and sliced

2 courgettes, sliced

2 carrots, sliced

2 celery sticks, sliced

2 potatoes, diced

400g/14oz can chopped tomatoes

5ml/1 tsp chilli powder

30ml/2 tbsp chopped fresh mint

15ml/1 tbsp ground cumin

400g/14oz can chick-peas, drained

salt and ground black pepper

mint sprigs, to garnish

1 Place the vegetable stock in a large microwaveproof casserole with the sliced pepper, courgettes, carrots and celery. Cover and microwave on HIGH for 2 minutes.

COOK'S TIP

Chick-peas are traditional in this type of Middle-Eastern dish, but if you prefer, red kidney or haricot beans can be used instead.

2 Add the potatoes, tomatoes, chilli powder, fresh mint, ground cumin and chick-peas to the vegetable dish and stir well. Cover the dish and microwave on HIGH for 15–20 minutes, remembering to stir twice during the cooking time.

3 Leave to stand, covered, for 5 minutes, until all the vegetables are tender. Season to taste with salt and pepper and serve hot, garnished with mint leaves.

VARIATION

Other vegetables can be substituted for those in the recipe, just use whatever you have to hand – try swede, sweet potato or parsnips.

Potato, Leek and Tomato Bake

This simple dish is delicious for lunch or supper – a real winner with all the family. Select the best tomatoes you can for a good flavour; if this means using small fruit, then add one or two extra.

Serves 4

675g/1½lb potatoes

2 leeks, trimmed and sliced

3 large tomatoes, sliced

a few fresh rosemary sprigs, crushed

1 garlic clove, crushed

300ml/½ pint/1¼ cups hot vegetable stock

15ml/1 tbsp olive oil

salt and ground black pepper

1 Scrub and thinly slice the potatoes. Then layer them with the leeks and tomatoes in a 1.2 litre/2 pint/5 cup microwave-proof dish that is suitable for grilling, scattering some rosemary between the layers and ending with a layer of potatoes.

2 Add the garlic to the stock, stir in salt and pepper to taste and pour over the vegetables. Brush the top layer of potatoes with the olive oil.

3 Cover and microwave on HIGH for 15–18 minutes or until the potatoes are tender. Leave to stand for 5 minutes, then remove the cover. Brown under a preheated hot grill, if liked, and serve hot.

COMBINATION MICROWAVE

This recipe is suitable for cooking in a combination microwave. Follow the oven manufacturer's timing guide for good results.

Summer Vegetable Braise

Tender, young vegetables are ideal for speedy cooking methods and the microwave ensures they stay tender-crisp.

INGREDIENTS

Serves 4

175g/6oz/2½ cups baby carrots

175g/6oz/2 cups sugar snap peas or
    mangetouts

115g/4oz/1¼ cups baby corn

90ml/6 tbsp vegetable stock

10ml/2 tsp lime juice

salt and black pepper

chopped fresh parsley and snipped fresh
    chives, to garnish

1 Place the carrots, peas and baby corn in a large microwaveproof bowl with the vegetable stock and lime juice.

2 Cover and microwave on HIGH for 7–9 minutes, stirring halfway through cooking, until the vegetables are just tender.

3 Season the vegetables to taste with salt and pepper, then stir in the chopped fresh parsley and snipped chives. Microwave on HIGH for 1 minute, until the vegetables are well flavoured with the herbs. Then serve at once.

VARIATION

To make a more substantial dish, tip the cooked vegetables into a gratin dish and top with a mixture of grated cheese and breadcrumbs, then grill until golden and bubbling.

COOK'S TIP

You can make this dish in the winter too, but cut larger, tougher vegetables into chunks and cook them for slightly longer.

Broccoli and Chestnut Terrine

Served hot or cold, this versatile terrine is equally suitable for a dinner party as for a picnic.

INGREDIENTS

Serves 4–6

450g/1lb broccoli, cut into small florets
60ml/4 tbsp water
225g/8oz cooked chestnuts,
    roughly chopped
50g/2oz/1 cup fresh wholemeal
    breadcrumbs
60ml/4 tbsp low-fat natural yogurt
30ml/2 tbsp freshly grated
    Parmesan cheese
salt and ground black pepper
grated nutmeg
2 eggs, beaten

1 Line a 900g/2lb glass loaf dish with clear film.

2 Place the broccoli in a microwaveproof bowl with the water. Cover and microwave on HIGH for 6 minutes, stirring once. Drain well. Reserve a quarter of the smallest florets and chop the rest finely.

3 Mix together the chestnuts, breadcrumbs, yogurt and Parmesan, adding seasoning and grated nutmeg to taste.

4 Fold in the chopped broccoli, reserved small florets and the beaten eggs.

5 Spoon the broccoli mixture into the prepared dish. Cover and microwave on HIGH for 3 minutes. Reduce the power setting to MEDIUM and microwave for a further 5–8 minutes, or until just firm and set. Leave to stand for 5 minutes.

6 Turn out the terrine on to a flat plate or tray. Serve cut into thick slices. New potatoes and salad are suitable accompaniments.

Salade Niçoise

INGREDIENTS

Serves 4

90ml/6 tbsp olive oil

30ml/2 tbsp tarragon vinegar

5ml/1 tsp tarragon or Dijon mustard

1 small garlic clove, crushed

12 small new or salad potatoes

115g/4oz/1 cup French beans

3–4 Little Gem lettuces, roughly chopped

200g/7oz can tuna in oil, drained

6 anchovy fillets, halved lengthways

12 black olives, stoned

4 tomatoes, chopped

4 spring onions, finely chopped

10ml/2 tsp capers

30ml/2 tbsp pine nuts

2 hard-boiled eggs, chopped

salt and ground black pepper

1 Mix the oil, vinegar, mustard, garlic and seasoning in a large salad bowl.

2 Place the potatoes in a microwaveproof bowl with 30ml/2 tbsp water. Cover and microwave on HIGH for 6–8 minutes, stirring halfway through cooking. Leave to stand, covered, for 3 minutes, then drain thoroughly.

3 Place the beans in a microwaveproof bowl with 15ml/1 tbsp water. Cover and microwave on HIGH for 3 minutes, stirring once. Leave to stand, covered, for 2 minutes, then drain.

4 Mix the potatoes and beans with the lettuce, tuna, anchovies, olives, tomatoes, spring onions and capers.

5 Just before serving, place the pine nuts on a small microwaveproof plate and microwave on HIGH for 3–4 minutes, stirring once every minute, until brown.

6 Sprinkle the pine nuts over the salad while still hot, add the eggs and toss all the ingredients together well. Serve with chunks of hot crusty bread.

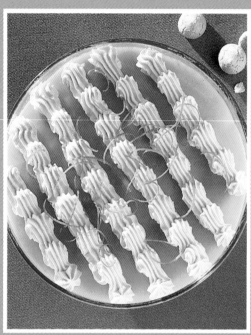

DESSERTS

Plum and Walnut Crumble

*Walnuts add a lovely crunch to the
fruit layer in this crumble –
almonds would be equally good.*

INGREDIENTS

Serves 4–6

1kg/2¼lb plums, halved and stoned

75g/3oz/¾ cup walnut pieces, toasted

175g/6oz/scant 1 cup demerara sugar

75g/3oz/6 tbsp butter or hard
    margarine, diced

175g/6oz/1½ cups plain flour

1 Butter a 1.2 litre/2 pint/5 cup
microwaveproof dish that is
suitable for grilling. Put the plums
in the dish, then stir in the nuts
and half the demerara sugar.

2 Rub the butter or margarine
into the flour until the
mixture resembles coarse crumbs.
Stir in the remaining sugar and
continue to rub in the fat until fine
crumbs are formed.

3 Cover the fruit with the
crumb mixture and press it
down lightly. Microwave the
crumble on HIGH for 14–16
minutes, rotating the dish three
times during cooking. Brown the
top under a preheated hot grill
until golden and crisp, if liked,
before serving.

VARIATION

To make Oat and Cinnamon
Crumble, substitute rolled oats for
half the flour in the crumble
mixture and add 2.5–5ml/½–1 tsp
ground cinnamon.

COMBINATION MICROWAVE

This recipe is suitable for cooking
in a combination microwave.
Follow your oven manufacturer's
timing guide for good results.

Gingerbread Upside-down Pudding

A proper pudding goes down well on a cold winter's day.

INGREDIENTS

Serves 4–6

sunflower oil, for brushing

15ml/1 tbsp soft brown sugar

8 walnut halves

4 medium peaches, halved and stoned, or canned peach halves

For the base

130g/4½oz/½ cup wholemeal flour

2.5ml/½ tsp bicarbonate of soda

7.5ml/1½ tsp ground ginger

5ml/1 tsp ground cinnamon

115g/4oz/½ cup molasses sugar

1 egg

120ml/4fl oz/½ cup skimmed milk

50ml/2fl oz/¼ cup sunflower oil

1 For the topping, brush the base and sides of a 23cm/9in round deep microwaveproof dish with oil. Line the base with grease-proof paper, oil the paper then sprinkle the base with sugar.

2 Place a walnut half in each peach half, then arrange the peaches cut-side down in the dish.

3 For the base, sift together the flour, bicarbonate of soda, ginger and cinnamon, then stir in the sugar. Beat together the egg, milk and oil, then mix into the dry ingredients until smooth.

4 Pour the mixture evenly over the peaches and microwave on MEDIUM for 6–8 minutes, or until the mixture has shrunk away from the sides of the dish, but the surface still looks wet. Leave to stand for 5 minutes. Turn out into a serving plate. Serve hot with yogurt or custard.

Spiced Pears in Cider

Serves 4

250ml/8fl oz/1 cup dry cider

thinly pared strip of lemon rind

1 cinnamon stick

30ml/2 tbsp soft brown sugar

4 firm pears

5ml/1 tsp arrowroot

15ml/1 tbsp water

ground cinnamon, to sprinkle

low-fat fromage frais, to serve

1 Place the cider, lemon rind, cinnamon stick and sugar in a microwaveproof bowl. Microwave on HIGH for 3–5 minutes until boiling, stirring frequently to dissolve the sugar. Meanwhile, peel the pears thinly, leaving them whole with the stems on.

2 Add the pears to the cider syrup. Spoon the syrup over the pears. Three-quarters cover the dish with clear film or with a lid. Microwave on HIGH for 5–6 minutes until the pears are just tender, turning and repositioning them in the bowl two or three times.

3 Carefully transfer the pears to another bowl using a slotted spoon. Microwave the cider syrup, uncovered, on HIGH for 15–17 minutes until it is reduced by half.

4 Mix the arrowroot with the water in a small bowl until smooth, then stir it into the syrup. Microwave on HIGH for 1 minute, stirring twice, until clear and thickened.

5 Pour the sauce over the pears and sprinkle with ground cinnamon. Leave to cool slightly, then serve warm with low-fat fromage frais.

VARIATIONS

Other fruits can be poached in this spicy liquid; try apples, peaches or nectarines. Cook the fruit whole or cut in half or quarters. The apples are best peeled before poaching, but you can cook the peaches and nectarines with their skins on.

COOK'S TIP

Any variety of pear can be used, but it is best to choose firm pears, or they will break up easily – Conference are a good choice.

Honey Fruit Yogurt Ice

INGREDIENTS

Serves 4–6

2 dessert apples, peeled, cored and finely
    chopped
4 ripe bananas, roughly chopped
15ml/1 tbsp lemon juice
30ml/2 tbsp clear honey
250g/9oz/1 cup Greek-style yogurt
2.5ml/½ tsp ground cinnamon
crisp biscuits, flaked hazelnuts and
    banana slices, to serve

1 Place the apples in a small
microwaveproof bowl,
cover and microwave on HIGH
for 2 minutes, stirring once.
Allow to cool.

2 Place the bananas in a food
processor or blender with the
lemon juice, honey, yogurt and
cinnamon. Process until smooth
and creamy. Add the cooked apples
and process briefly to mix.

3 Pour the mixture into a freezer
container and freeze until
almost solid. Spoon back into the
food processor and process again
until smooth.

4 Return to the freezer until
firm. Allow to soften at room
temperature for 15 minutes, then
serve in scoops, with crisp biscuits,
flaked hazelnuts and banana slices.

Autumn Pudding

INGREDIENTS

Serves 6

10 slices bread, at least one day old
1 Bramley cooking apple, peeled, cored
    and sliced
225g/8oz ripe red plums, halved
    and stoned
225g/8oz blackberries
60ml/4 tbsp water
75g/3oz/6 tbsp caster sugar

1 Remove the crusts from the
bread and stamp out a 7.5cm/
3in round from one slice. Cut the
remaining bread in half.

2 Place the bread round in the
base of a 1.2 litre/2 pint/5 cup
pudding basin, then overlap the
fingers around the sides, saving
some for the top.

3 Mix the apple, plums, blackberries, water and caster sugar
in a microwaveproof bowl. Cover
and microwave on HIGH for 7–8
minutes or until the sugar
dissolves, the juices begin to flow
and the fruit softens. Stir twice
during cooking.

4 Reserve the juice and spoon
the fruit into the bread-lined
basin. Top with the reserved bread,
then spoon over the reserved
fruit juices.

5 Cover the basin with a saucer
and place weights on top.
Chill the pudding overnight. Turn
out on to a serving plate and
serve with low-fat yogurt or
fromage frais.

Tangerine Trifle

An unusual variation on a traditional trifle – of course, you can add a little alcohol if you wish.

INGREDIENTS

Serves 4

5 trifle sponges, halved lengthways

30ml/2 tbsp apricot conserve

15-20 ratafia biscuits

142g/4¾oz packet tangerine jelly

300g/11oz can mandarin oranges, drained, juice reserved

600ml/1 pint/2½ cups prepared custard

whipped cream and shreds of orange rind, to decorate

caster sugar, for sprinkling

1 Spread the halved sponge cakes with apricot conserve and arrange them in the base of a deep serving bowl or glass dish. Sprinkle over the ratafia biscuits.

2 Break up the jelly into a microwaveproof jug, add the juice from the canned mandarins and microwave on HIGH for 2 minutes, then stir to dissolve the jelly.

3 Make up the jelly to 600ml/1 pint/2½ cups with ice-cold water, stir well and leave to cool for up to 30 minutes. Scatter the mandarin oranges over the cakes and ratafias.

4 Pour the jelly over the mandarin oranges, cake and ratafias and chill for 1 hour, or until the jelly has set.

5 Pour the custard over the trifle and chill again. When ready to serve, pipe the whipped cream over the custard. Place the orange rind shreds in a sieve and rinse under cold water, then sprinkle them with caster sugar and use to decorate the trifle.

Baked Apples with Apricots

INGREDIENTS

Serves 6

75g/3oz/½ cup ready-to-eat dried
   apricots, chopped

50g/2oz/½ cup walnuts, chopped

5ml/1 tsp grated lemon rind

2.5ml/½ tsp ground cinnamon

80g/3½oz/½ cup soft light brown sugar

15g/1oz/2 tbsp butter, at
   room temperature

6 large eating apples

15ml/1 tbsp melted butter

120ml/4fl oz/½ cup water or fruit juice

1 Place the apricots, walnuts, lemon rind and cinnamon in a bowl. Add the sugar and butter and stir until thoroughly mixed.

2 Core the apples, without cutting all the way through to the base. Peel the top of each apple and slightly widen the top of each opening to make plenty of room for the filling.

3 Spoon the filling into the apples, packing it down lightly into their middles.

4 Place the stuffed apples in a microwaveproof dish large enough to hold them neatly side by side.

5 Brush the apples with the melted butter and pour the water or fruit juice around them. Microwave on HIGH for 9–10 minutes, rearranging halfway through cooking, until the apples are tender. Serve hot.

BAKING

Sage Soda Bread

This wonderful loaf, quite unlike bread made with yeast, has a velvety texture and a powerful sage aroma.

INGREDIENTS

Makes 1 loaf

350g/12oz/3 cups wholemeal flour

115g/4oz/1 cup strong white flour

5ml/1 tsp salt

10ml/2 tsp bicarbonate of soda

30ml/2 tbsp shredded fresh sage

300–450ml/½–¾ pint/1¼–1¾ cups buttermilk

1 Sift the dry ingredients into a large mixing bowl.

2 Stir in the sage and add enough buttermilk to make a soft dough.

3 Shape the dough into a round loaf and place on a lightly oiled plate and cut a deep cross in the top.

4 Microwave on MEDIUM for 5 minutes, give the plate a half turn and microwave on HIGH for a further 3 minutes. Brown the top under a preheated hot grill, if liked. Allow to stand for 10 minutes, then transfer to a wire rack to cool. Best eaten on the day of making.

COMBINATION MICROWAVE

This recipe is suitable for cooking in a combination microwave. Follow the oven manufacturer's timing guide for good results.

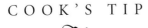

COOK'S TIP

As an alternative to the sage, try using finely chopped rosemary.

Cheese and Marjoram Scones

INGREDIENTS

Makes 18

115g/4oz/1 cup wholemeal flour

115g/4oz/1 cup self-raising flour

pinch of salt

40g/1½oz/3 tbsp butter

1.5ml/¼ tsp dry mustard

10ml/2 tsp dried marjoram

50–75g/2–3oz/½–⅔ cup Cheddar cheese,
    finely grated

about 125ml/4fl oz/½ cup milk

50g/2oz/⅓ cup pecans or walnuts,
    chopped

1 Sift the two types of flour into a bowl and add the salt. Cut the butter into small pieces, and rub it into the flour until the mixture resembles fine bread-crumbs.

2 Add the mustard, marjoram and grated cheese, then mix in sufficient milk to make a soft dough. Knead the dough lightly.

3 Roll out the dough on a floured surface to about a 2cm/¾in thickness and cut out about 18 scones using a 5cm/2in square cutter.

4 Brush the scones with a little milk and sprinkle the chopped pecans or walnuts over the top. Place the scones on a piece of non-stick parchment in the microwave, spacing them well apart. Microwave on HIGH for 3–3½ minutes, repositioning the scones twice during cooking.

5 Insert a skewer into the centre of each scone: if it comes out clean, the scone is cooked. Return any uncooked scones to the microwave and microwave on HIGH for a further 30 seconds. Brown under a preheated hot grill until golden, if liked. Serve warm, split and buttered.

VARIATION

For Herb and Mustard Scones, use 30ml/2 tbsp chopped fresh parsley or chives instead of the dried marjoram and 5ml/1 tsp Dijon mustard instead of the dry mustard. Substitute 50g/2oz chopped pistachio nuts for the pecans or walnuts.

Oat Florentines

These irresistible "bakes" make the best of familiar flapjacks and old-fashioned, chocolate-coated florentine biscuits.

INGREDIENTS

Makes 16

75g/3oz/6 tbsp butter

45ml/3 tbsp/¼ cup golden syrup

115g/4oz/1¼ cups rolled oats

25g/1oz/2 tbsp soft brown sugar

25g/1oz/2 tbsp chopped mixed
   candied peel

25g/1oz/2 tbsp glacé cherries,
   coarsely chopped

25g/1oz/¼ cup hazelnuts,
   coarsely chopped

115g/4oz/⅔ cup plain chocolate

1 Lightly grease a 20cm/8in square microwaveproof shallow dish and line the base with a sheet of rice paper.

2 Place the butter and golden syrup in a microwaveproof bowl and microwave on HIGH for 1½ minutes to melt. Stir well.

3 Add the oats, sugar, peel, cherries and hazelnuts, mixing well to blend.

4 Spoon the mixture into the dish and level the surface with the back of a spoon. Microwave on MEDIUM HIGH for 6 minutes, giving the dish a half turn every 2 minutes. Allow to cool slightly then cut into 16 fingers and place on a wire rack to cool.

5 Break the chocolate into pieces and place in a microwaveproof bowl. Microwave on HIGH for 2–3 minutes, stirring twice, until melted and smooth. Spread over the tops of the florentines and mark in a zig-zag pattern with the prongs of a fork. Leave to set.

COOK'S TIP

Rice paper is used for cooking in traditional recipes as well as in microwave methods. It prevents mixtures, such as this sweet oat base, from sticking by cooking on to them. When cooked, the rice paper can be eaten with the biscuits or other items.

Blueberry Crumble Tea Bread

INGREDIENTS

Makes 8 pieces

50g/2oz/4 tbsp butter or margarine, at
   room temperature

175g/6oz/²⁄₃ cup caster sugar

1 egg, at room temperature

120ml/4fl oz/½ cup milk

225g/8oz/2 cups plain flour

10ml/2 tsp baking powder

2.5ml/½ tsp salt

275g/10oz fresh blueberries or bilberries

For the topping

115g/4oz sugar

40g/1½oz/6 tbsp plain flour

2.5ml/½ tsp ground cinnamon

50g/2oz/4 tbsp butter, cut in pieces

1 Grease a 23 x 18cm/9 x 7in microwaveproof dish.

2 Cream the butter or margarine with the caster sugar until light and fluffy. Beat in the egg, then mix in the milk.

3 Sift over the flour, baking powder and salt and stir just enough to blend the ingredients.

4 Add the berries and stir them in lightly. Spoon the mixture into the prepared dish.

5 For the topping, place the sugar, flour, ground cinnamon and butter in a mixing bowl. Rub in the butter until the mixture resembles coarse breadcrumbs; alternatively, cut in the butter with a pastry blender.

6 Sprinkle the topping over the mixture in the baking dish. Microwave on MEDIUM for 12 minutes, rotating the dish twice during cooking. Brown under a preheated hot grill, if liked. Leave to stand for 5 minutes. Serve warm or cold.

Maple and Banana Tea Bread

Serves 8–10

115g/4oz/1 cup wholemeal flour

5ml/1 tsp bicarbonate of soda

2 bananas, mashed

60ml/4 tbsp natural yogurt

50g/2oz/4 tbsp soft light brown sugar

65g/2½oz/5 tbsp unsalted butter

1 egg, beaten

30ml/2 tbsp maple syrup

75g/3oz/½ cup dried dates,
    coarsely chopped

icing sugar, to dust

1 Lightly grease a 23 x 13cm/
9 x 5in microwaveproof loaf
dish and line the base with greaseproof paper.

2 Sift the wholemeal flour with
the bicarbonate of soda,
adding the bran left in the sieve.

3 Mix the bananas with the
yogurt, brown sugar, butter,
egg and syrup, blending well. Add
the flour mixture and dates and
mix into a smooth batter. Spoon
the mixture evenly into the loaf
dish and spread it out slightly.

4 To prevent the ends of the
cake from over-cooking, wrap
a 5cm/2in wide strip of smooth
foil over each end of the dish. Place
the dish on an inverted plate in the
oven and microwave on MEDIUM
for 10 minutes, giving the dish a
quarter turn every 2½ minutes.

5 Increase the power setting to
HIGH and microwave for a
further 2 minutes. Remove the foil,
give the dish a quarter turn and
microwave for 1–3 minutes more,
until the tea bread shrinks from
the sides of the dish. Leave to stand
for 10 minutes before turning out
to cool on a wire rack.

6 Sift a light coating of icing
sugar over the top of the cake
before serving. Serve warm or cold.

Hot Chocolate Cake

This is wonderfully wicked, either hot as a pudding, to serve with a white chocolate sauce, or cold as a cake. The basic cake freezes well – thaw, then warm it in the microwave before serving.

INGREDIENTS

Makes 10–12 slices

200g/7oz/1¾ cups self-raising
   wholemeal flour
25g/1oz/¼ cup cocoa powder
pinch of salt
175g/6oz/¾ cup soft margarine
175g/6oz/¾ cup soft light brown sugar
few drops vanilla essence
4 eggs
75g/3oz white chocolate, roughly chopped
chocolate leaves and curls, to decorate

For the white chocolate sauce
75g/3oz white chocolate
150ml/¼ pint/⅔ cup single cream
30–40ml/2–3 tbsp milk

1 Sift the flour, cocoa powder and salt into a bowl, adding the bran from the sieve.

2 Cream the margarine, sugar and vanilla essence together until light and fluffy, then gently beat in one egg.

3 Gradually stir in the remaining eggs, one at a time, alternately folding in some of the flour, until all the flour mixture is well blended in.

4 Stir in the white chocolate and spoon the mixture into a 675–900g/1½–2lb greased microwaveproof loaf dish. Shield each end of the dish with a small piece of smooth foil, shiny side in. Cover with clear film and microwave on HIGH for 8–9 minutes, giving the dish a quarter turn three or four times during cooking. Remove the clear film and foil for the last 1½ minutes of the cooking time. The cake is cooked when a skewer inserted in the centre comes out clean. Leave to stand while making the sauce.

5 Place the chocolate and cream for the sauce in a microwave-proof bowl and microwave on MEDIUM for 2–3 minutes, until the chocolate has melted. Add the milk and stir until cool.

6 Serve the cake sliced, in a pool of sauce, decorated with chocolate leaves and curls.

COMBINATION MICROWAVE

This recipe is suitable for cooking in a combination microwave. Follow your oven manufacturer's timing guide for good results.

Coconut Pyramids

Without the danger of using a conventional cooker, making a batch of these all-time favourites is an ideal wet-afternoon occupation for young children.

Makes about 15

225g/8oz/1 cup unsweetened desiccated coconut

115g/4oz/½ cup caster sugar

2 egg whites

oil, for greasing

1 Mix together the desiccated coconut and sugar. Lightly whisk the egg whites. Fold enough egg white into the coconut to make a fairly firm mixture. You may not need quite all the egg whites.

2 Form the mixture into pyramid shapes by taking a teaspoonful and rolling it first into a ball. Flatten the base and press the top into a point. Arrange the pyramids on greaseproof paper, leaving space between them.

3 Microwave on HIGH for 2–3 minutes or until the pyramids are just firm, but still soft inside. Transfer to a baking sheet and place under a preheated hot grill to tinge the tops golden, if liked.

COOK'S TIP

To freeze biscuits, arrange in a single layer on a tray. When hard, pack in bags or boxes. Thaw for 1 hour before use.

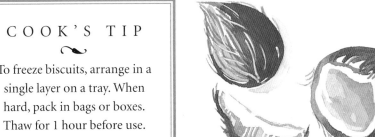

4 Slide a palette knife under the pyramids to loosen them, and leave to cool before removing from the baking sheet.

COOKING AND DEFROSTING CHARTS

Cooking Fish and Shellfish

COD
steamed steaks and fillets

450g/1lb fillets · 2 x 225g/8oz steaks · 4 x 225g/8oz steaks · HIGH

Arrange fish fillets in a microwaveproof dish so that the thinner tail ends are to the centre. Fold in any flaps of skin on steaks and secure with wooden cocktail sticks. Dot with a little butter, sprinkle with seasoning and add a dash of lemon juice. Cover and microwave for 5–7 minutes for 450g/1lb fillets; 5 minutes for 2 x 225g/8oz steaks; and 8–9 minutes for 4 x 225g/8oz steaks, rearranging once halfway through cooking. Leave to stand, covered, for 3 minutes before serving.

FISH CAKES

4 x 75g/3oz · HIGH

Place in a shallow microwaveproof dish and brush with a little melted butter if liked. Microwave for 5 minutes, turning over once, halfway through cooking. Times refer to chilled or fresh fish cakes (thaw frozen fish cakes before cooking). Leave to stand for 2–3 minutes before serving. If liked, the fish cakes can be cooked in a preheated browning dish.

FISH FINGERS

2 · 4 · 6 · 8 · 12 · HIGH

For best results cook in a preheated browning dish. Microwave for 1½ minutes for 2; 2 minutes for 4; 3 minutes for 6; 4 minutes for 8; and 5 minutes for 12 fish fingers, turning over once, halfway through cooking. Times refer to frozen fish fingers. Leave to stand for 1–2 minutes before serving.

FISH ROES

115g/4oz · 225g/8oz · LOW

Rinse the fish roes and place in a microwaveproof dish with a large knob of butter and seasoning to taste. Cover and microwave for 4–4½ minutes for 115g/4oz; and 6–8 minutes for 225g/8oz fish roes, stirring once halfway through cooking. Leave to stand, covered, for 2 minutes before serving.

HADDOCK
steamed steaks and fillets

450g/1lb fillets · 2 x 225g/8oz steaks · 4 x 225g/8oz steaks · HIGH

Arrange the fish fillets in a microwaveproof dish so that the thinner tail ends are to the centre. Fold in any flaps of skin on steaks and secure with wooden cocktail sticks. Dot with a little butter, sprinkle with seasoning and add a dash of lemon juice. Cover and microwave for 5–7 minutes for 450g/1lb fillets; 5 minutes for 2 x 225g/8oz steaks; and 8–9 minutes for 4 x 225g/8oz steaks, rearranging once halfway through cooking. Leave to stand, covered, for 3 minutes before serving.

HALIBUT
steaks

2 x 225g/8oz steaks · HIGH

Fold in any flaps of skin and secure with wooden cocktail sticks. Place in a shallow microwaveproof dish and dot with a little butter. Season with salt, pepper and lemon juice. Cover and microwave for 4–5 minutes. Leave to stand, covered, for 2–3 minutes before serving.

HERRING
fresh whole

per 450g/1lb · HIGH

Remove heads and clean and gut before cooking. Slash the skin in several places to prevent bursting during cooking. Place in a shallow microwaveproof dish and season to taste. Shield the tail ends of the fish if liked. Cover with greaseproof paper and microwave for 3–4 minutes per 450g/1lb, turning over once halfway through cooking. Leave to stand, covered, for 2–3 minutes before serving.

KIPPERS
fillets

2 · 4 · 8 · HIGH

If buying whole fish then remove heads and tails. Place skin-side down in a shallow microwaveproof cooking dish. Cover loosely and microwave for 1–2 minutes for 2 fillets; 3–4 minutes for 4 fillets; and 6–7 minutes for 8 fillets, rearranging once halfway through cooking. Leave to stand, covered, for 2–3 minutes before serving.

LOBSTER
to reheat cooked whole lobster and tails

450g/1lb whole · 450g/1lb tails · HIGH

Place in a shallow microwaveproof dish and cover loosely. Microwave for 6–8 minutes for 450g/1lb whole; and 5–6 minutes for 450g/1lb tails, turning over once halfway through cooking. Leave to stand, covered, for 5 minutes before serving.

MACKEREL			
fresh whole	per 450g/1lb	HIGH	Remove heads and clean and gut before cooking. Slash the skin in several places to prevent bursting during cooking. Place in a shallow microwaveproof dish and season to taste. Shield the tail ends of the fish if liked. Cover with greaseproof paper and microwave for 3–4 minutes per 450g/1lb, turning over once halfway through cooking. Leave to stand, covered, for 2–3 minutes before serving.
MUSSELS			
fresh steamed	675g/1½lb	HIGH	Sort the mussels and scrub thoroughly with cold running water. Place in a microwaveproof dish with 75ml/5 tbsp water, fish stock or dry white wine. Cover loosely and microwave for 5 minutes, stirring once halfway through cooking. Remove with a slotted spoon, discarding any mussels that do not open. Thicken the cooking juices with a little beurre manié, (butter and flour paste), if liked, to serve with the mussels.
PLAICE			
steamed fillets	450g/1lb fillets	HIGH	Arrange fish fillets in a microwaveproof dish so that the thinner tail ends are to the centre of the dish. Dot with a little butter, sprinkle with seasoning and add a dash of lemon juice. Cover and microwave for 4–6 minutes, rearranging once halfway through cooking. Leave to stand, covered, for 3 minutes before serving.
RED OR GREY MULLET			
fresh whole	2 x 250g/9oz 4 x 250g/9oz	HIGH	Clean and gut before cooking. Place in a shallow microwaveproof dish and slash the skin in several places to prevent bursting during cooking. Cover and microwave for 4–5 minutes for 2 x 250g/9oz mullet; and 8–9 minutes for 4 x 250g/9oz mullet, turning over once halfway through cooking. Leave to stand, covered, for 5 minutes before serving.
SALMON			
steamed steaks	2 x 225g/8oz 4 x 225g/8oz	HIGH	Place in a shallow microwaveproof dish so that the narrow ends are to the centre of the dish. Dot with butter and sprinkle with lemon juice and salt and pepper. Cover with greaseproof paper and microwave for 2½–3 minutes for 2 x 225g/8oz steaks; and 4½–5¾ minutes for 4 x 225g/8oz steaks, turning over once halfway through cooking. Leave to stand, covered, for 5 minutes before serving.
	4 x 175g/6oz steaks	MEDIUM	Prepare and cook as above but use MEDIUM power and allow 10½–11½ minutes.
whole salmon and salmon trout	450g/1lb 900g/2lb 1.5kg/3–3½lb 1.75kg/4–4½lb	HIGH	Remove the head if liked. Slash or prick the skin in several places to prevent bursting during cooking. Place in a microwaveproof dish with 150ml/¼ pint/⅔ cup boiling water and a dash of lemon juice. Cover and microwave for 4½–5 minutes for a 450g/1lb fish, 8½–10½ minutes for a 900g/2lb fish; 11–14½ minutes for a 1.5kg/3–3½lb fish; and 14½–18½ minutes for a 1.75kg/4–4½lb fish, rotating 3 times during cooking. Leave to stand, covered, for 5 minutes before serving.
SCALLOPS			
steamed fresh	450g/1lb	MEDIUM	Remove from their shells. Place in a shallow microwaveproof dish and cover with absorbent kitchen paper. Microwave for 8–12 minutes, rearranging once, halfway through cooking. Leave to stand, covered, for 3 minutes before serving.
SHRIMPS AND PRAWNS			
to boil	450g/1lb 900g/2lb	HIGH	Rinse and place in a microwaveproof dish with 600ml/1 pint/2½ cups water, a dash of vinegar or lemon juice and a bay leaf if liked. Cover and microwave for 6–8 minutes for 450g/1lb; 8–10 minutes for 900g/2lb, stirring once halfway through cooking. Leave to stand, covered, for 3 minutes before draining and shelling.

SOLE			
steamed fillets	450g/1lb	HIGH	Arrange fish fillets in a microwaveproof dish so that the thinner tail ends are to the centre of the dish. Dot with a little butter, season and add a dash of lemon juice. Cover and microwave for 4–6 minutes, rearranging once half-way through cooking. Leave to stand, covered, for 3 minutes before serving.
SMOKED HADDOCK			
steamed fillets	450g/1lb	HIGH	Arrange fish fillets in a microwaveproof dish so that the thinner tail ends are to the centre of the dish. Dot with butter, sprinkle with seasoning and add a dash of lemon juice. Cover and microwave for 5–6 minutes, rearranging once halfway through cooking. Leave the fish to stand, covered, for 3 minutes before serving.
poached fillets	450g/1lb	HIGH	Place the fillets in a shallow microwaveproof dish with the thinner tail ends to the centre. Pour over 120ml/4fl oz/½ cup milk, dot with a little butter and season to taste. Cover and microwave for 5–6 minutes, rearranging once halfway through cooking. Leave to stand, covered, for 3 minutes before serving.
TROUT			
whole	2 x 250g/9oz 4 x 250g/9oz	HIGH	Clean and gut before cooking. Place in a shallow microwaveproof dish. Slash the skin in several places to prevent bursting during cooking. Dot with butter if liked and season to taste. Cover and microwave for 4–5 minutes for 2 x 250g/9oz trout; and 8–9 minutes for 4 x 250g/9oz trout, turning over once halfway through cooking. Leave the fish to stand, covered, for 5 minutes before serving.
WHITING			
steamed fillets	450g/1lb	HIGH	Arrange fish fillets in a microwaveproof dish so that the thinner tail ends are to the centre of the dish. Dot with a little butter, sprinkle with seasoning and add a dash or two of lemon juice. Cover and microwave for 4–6 minutes, rearranging once halfway through cooking. Leave to stand, covered, for 3 minutes before serving.

Cooking Poultry and Game

CHICKEN

whole roast fresh chicken	1kg/2¼lb 1.5kg/3–3½lb 1.75kg/4–4½lb	HIGH	Rinse, dry and truss the chicken into a neat shape. Season and calculate the cooking time after weighing (and stuffing). Cook breast-side down for half of the cooking time and breast-side up for the remaining cooking time. Brush with a browning agent if liked and shield the wing tips with foil if necessary. Microwave for 12–16 minutes for a 1kg/2¼lb chicken; 18–24 minutes for a 1.5kg/3–3½lb chicken; 25–36 minutes for a 1.75kg/4–4½lb chicken. Cover with foil and leave to stand for 10–15 minutes before carving.
portions	1 x 225g/8oz portion 2 x 225g/8oz portions 4 x 225g/8oz portions	HIGH	Prick with a fork and brush with a browning agent if liked. Alternatively, crisp and brown under a preheated hot grill after cooking. Cover with buttered greaseproof paper to cook. Microwave for 5–7 minutes for 225g/8oz portion; 10–12 minutes for 2 x 225g/8oz portions; 18–24 minutes for 4 x 225g/8oz portions. Leave to stand, covered, for 5–10 minutes before serving.
drumsticks	2 4 8	HIGH	Prick with a fork and brush with a browning agent if liked. Alternatively, crisp and brown under a preheated hot grill after cooking. Cover with buttered greaseproof paper to cook. Microwave for 3–5 minutes for 2 drumsticks; 8–9 minutes for 4 drumsticks; 16–19 minutes for 8 drumsticks. Leave to stand, covered, for 5–10 minutes before serving.
thighs	8	HIGH	Prick with a fork and brush with a browning agent if liked. Alternatively, crisp and brown under a preheated hot grill after cooking. Cover with buttered greaseproof paper to cook. Microwave 8 thighs for 17–20 minutes. Leave to stand, covered, for 5–10 minutes before serving.
breasts	2 4	HIGH	Prick with a fork and brush with a browning agent if liked. Alternatively, crisp and brown under a preheated hot grill after cooking. Cover with buttered greaseproof paper to cook. Microwave for 2–3 minutes for 2 breasts; 3½–4 minutes for 4 breasts. Leave to stand, covered, for 5–10 minutes before serving.
livers, fresh or thawed frozen	225g/8oz 450g/1lb	HIGH	Rinse well and prick to prevent bursting during cooking. Place in a microwaveproof dish with a knob of butter. Cover loosely and microwave for 2–3 minutes for 225g/8oz; and 5–6 minutes for 450g/1lb, stirring twice during cooking. Leave to stand for 2 minutes before serving or using.

DUCK

whole roast fresh duck	1.75kg/4–4½lb 2.25kg/5–5¼lb per 450g/1lb	HIGH	Rinse, dry and truss the duck into a neat shape, securing any tail-end flaps of skin to the main body. Prick thoroughly and place on a rack or upturned saucer in a microwaveproof dish for cooking. Cook breast-side down for half of the cooking time, and breast-side up for the remaining cooking time. Microwave for 28–32 minutes for a 1.75kg/4–4½lb duck; 35–40 minutes for a 2.25kg/5–5¼lb duck; or calculate times at 7–8 minutes per 450g/1lb. Drain away excess fat 3 times during cooking and shield tips, tail end and legs with foil if necessary. Cover with foil and leave to stand for 10–15 minutes before serving. Crisp the skin under a preheated hot grill if liked.

GAME BIRDS

whole roast	1 x 450g/1lb 2 x 450g/1lb 1 x 900g/2lb 2 x 900g/2lb	HIGH	Rinse, dry and truss the birds into a neat shape. Brush with a browning agent if liked. Cover with greaseproof paper to cook. Microwave for 9–10 minutes for 450g/1lb bird; 18–22 minutes for 2 x 450g/1lb birds; 20–22 minutes for 900g/2lb bird; and 35–40 minutes for 2 x 900g/2lb birds, turning over twice during cooking. Leave to stand, covered, for 5 minutes before serving.

TURKEY

whole roast fresh	2.75kg/6lb 4kg/9lb 5.5kg/12lb larger birds over 5.5kg/12lb *per* *450g/1lb*	HIGH	Rinse, dry and stuff the turkey if liked. Truss into a neat shape and weigh to calculate the cooking time. Brush with melted butter or browning agent if liked. Divide the cooking time into quarters and cook breast-side down for the first quarter, on one side for the second quarter, on the remaining side for the third quarter and breast-side up for the final quarter. Shield any parts that start to cook faster than others with small strips of foil. Microwave for 42 minutes for a 2.75kg/6lb bird; 63 minutes for a 4kg/9lb bird; 84 minutes for a 5.5kg/12lb bird; or allow 7 minutes per 450g/1lb for larger birds. When cooked, cover with foil and leave to stand for 10–25 minutes (depending upon size of bird) before carving.
drumsticks	2 x 350g/12oz	HIGH *then* MEDIUM	Place on a roasting rack, meaty sections downwards. Baste with a browning agent if liked. Cover and microwave on HIGH for 5 minutes, then on MEDIUM for 13–15 minutes, turning once. Leave to stand, covered, for 5 minutes before serving.
breasts	2 x 225g/8oz breasts 4 x 225g/8oz breasts	MEDIUM	Beat out flat if preferred and place in a shallow dish. Baste with browning agent if liked. Microwave for 8–10 minutes for 2 x 225g/8oz breasts; and 16–18 minutes for 4 x 225g/8oz breasts, turning over once. Leave to stand for 2–3 minutes before serving.

Cooking Meat

BACON

back and streaky rashers	4 rashers 450g/1lb	HIGH	Place small quantities between sheets of kitchen paper, larger quantities on a plate or microwaveproof bacon rack covered with kitchen paper. Microwave for 3½–4 minutes for 4 rashers; and 12–14 minutes for 450g/1lb, turning over once. Leave to stand for 1–2 minutes before serving.
joint	900g/2lb joint	HIGH	Remove any skin and score the fat into a diamond pattern. Sprinkle with a little brown sugar and stud with cloves if liked. Place on a microwaveproof roasting rack or upturned saucer in a dish. Microwave for 20–24 minutes, rotating the dish twice. Leave to stand, covered with foil, for 10–15 minutes before serving.

BEEF

roast joint	per 450g/1lb	HIGH *then* MEDIUM	Ideally place the joint on a microwaveproof roasting rack or upturned saucer inside a roasting bag. Calculate the cooking time according to weight and microwave on HIGH for the first 5 minutes then on MEDIUM for the remaining time. Turn the joint over halfway through the cooking time.

per 450g/1lb
topside or sirloin (boned and rolled)

rare	8–9 minutes
medium	11–12 minutes
well done	15–16 minutes

forerib or back rib (on the bone)

rare	7–8 minutes
medium	13–14 minutes
well done	15 minutes

forerib or back rib (boned and rolled)

rare	11–12 minutes
medium	13–14 minutes
well done	15–16 minutes

Cover with foil after cooking and leave to stand for 10–15 minutes before carving.

minced beef	450g/1lb	HIGH	Place in a microwaveproof dish, cover and microwave for 10–12 minutes, breaking up and stirring twice.
hamburgers	1 x 115g/4oz 2 x 115g/4oz 3 x 115g/4oz 4 x 115g/4oz	HIGH	Ideally cook in a preheated browning dish. If this isn't possible then cook on a roasting rack and increase the times slightly. Microwave for 2½–3 minutes for 1; 3½–4 minutes for 2; 4½–5 minutes for 3; and 5–5½ minutes for 4, turning over once halfway through the cooking time. Leave to stand for 2–3 minutes before serving.
meatloaf	450g/1lb loaf	HIGH	Place your favourite 450g/1lb seasoned beef mixture in a microwaveproof loaf dish, packing in firmly and levelling the surface. Microwave for 7 minutes, allow to stand for 5 minutes, then microwave for a further 5 minutes. Leave to stand, covered with foil, for 3 minutes before serving.
steaks	2 x 225g/8oz rump, sirloin or fillet steaks 4 x 225g/8oz rump, sirloin or fillet steaks	HIGH	Cook with or without the use of a browning dish. If cooking without, then brush with a browning agent if liked prior to cooking. Place in a lightly oiled microwaveproof dish and turn over halfway through the cooking time. Microwave for 5–5½ minutes for 2 x 225g/8oz steaks; and 7½–8½ minutes for 4 x 225g/8oz steaks.

If using a browning dish then preheat first, add a little oil and brush to coat the base. Add the steaks, pressing down well. Turn the steaks over halfway through the cooking time. Microwave for 2¼–2½ minutes for 2 x 225g/8oz steaks; and 3½–4 minutes for 4 x 225g/8oz steaks. Leave to stand for 1–2 minutes before serving.

GAMMON

braised steaks	4 x 115g/4oz steaks	HIGH	Remove the rind and scissor-snip the fat off the gammon steaks. Place in a large shallow microwaveproof dish. Add 150ml/¼ pint/⅔ cup wine, cider or fruit juice (and marinate for 1 hour if liked). Microwave for 4 minutes, rearranging once. Leave to stand, covered, for 5 minutes before serving.
raw joint	per 450g/1lb	HIGH	Place in a pierced roasting bag in a microwaveproof dish. Microwave for 12–14 minutes per 450g/1lb, turning over halfway through the cooking time. Cover with foil and leave to stand for 10 minutes before carving.

KIDNEYS

fresh lamb's, pig's or ox	115g/4oz 225g/8oz 450g/1lb	HIGH	Halve and core the kidneys. Preheat a browning dish. Add 5ml/1 tsp oil and the kidneys. Microwave for 4 minutes for 115g/4oz; 6–8 minutes for 225g/8oz; and 12–15 minutes for 450g/1lb, turning and rearranging twice. Leave to stand, covered, for 3 minutes before serving.

LAMB

roast joint	per 450g/1lb	HIGH *then* MEDIUM	Place the joint on a microwaveproof roasting rack or upturned saucer inside a dish and shield any thin or vulnerable areas with a little foil. Calculate the cooking time according to weight and microwave on HIGH for the first 5 minutes, then on MEDIUM for the remaining time. Turn the joint over halfway through the cooking time.

per 450g/1lb

leg joint with bone

rare	8–10 minutes
medium	10–12 minutes
well done	12–14 minutes

boned leg joints

rare	10–12 minutes
medium	13–15 minutes
well done	16–18 minutes

shoulder joints

rare	7–9 minutes
medium	9–11 minutes
well done	11–13 minutes

chops and steaks	2 loin chops 4 loin chops 2 chump chops 4 chump chops	HIGH	Brush with a browning agent if liked, or cook in a browning dish. Microwave for 6–7 minutes for 2 loin chops; 8–9 minutes for 4 loin chops; 6–8 minutes for 2 chump chops; and 8–10 minutes for 4 chump chops, turning over halfway through the cooking time. Leave to stand for 2–3 minutes before serving.
rack	1.2kg/2–2½lb rack with 7 ribs	HIGH	Chop rack in half and place both pieces together, bones interleaved guard-of-honour style, then tie in place. Place on a microwaveproof roasting rack. Microwave for 12 minutes for rare; 13 minutes for medium; and 14½–15 minutes for well-done lamb, rotating the dish every 3 minutes. Cover with foil and leave to stand for 10 minutes before carving.

LIVER

fresh lamb's liver	450g/1lb	HIGH	Preheat a browning dish. Add 15ml/1 tbsp oil and 15g/½oz/1 tbsp butter. Add sliced, washed and dried liver, pressing down well. Microwave for 1 minute, turn over and microwave for a further 4–5 minutes, rearranging once. Leave to stand for 2 minutes before serving.

PORK

roast joint	per 450g/1lb	HIGH *or* MEDIUM	Place the joint in a microwaveproof dish on a rack if possible. Times are given for roasting on HIGH or MEDIUM. Both methods work well but the latter tends to give a crisper crackling. Turn the joint over halfway through cooking. Brown and crisp under a preheated hot grill after cooking if liked and before the standing time. Calculate the cooking time according to weight and microwave for: *per 450g/1lb* loin, leg and hand joints on bone HIGH 8–9 minutes *or* MEDIUM 12–14 minutes loin and leg joints (boned) HIGH 8–10 minutes *or* MEDIUM 13–15 minutes Cover with foil after cooking and leave to stand for 10–20 minutes before carving.
chops	2 loin chops 4 loin chops 2 chump chops 4 chump chops	HIGH	Brush with a browning agent if liked, or cook in a browning dish. Microwave for 4–5 minutes for 2 loin chops; 6–8 minutes for 4 loin chops; 8–10 minutes for 2 chump chops; and 11–13 minutes for 4 chump chops, turning over once halfway through cooking. Leave to stand for 5 minutes before serving.
pork fillet or tenderloin	350g/12oz	HIGH *then* MEDIUM	Shield the narrow, thin ends of the fillet with a little foil. Place on a microwaveproof roasting rack or upturned saucer in a dish. Microwave on HIGH for 3 minutes, then on MEDIUM for 10–15 minutes, turning over once. Leave to stand, covered with foil, for 5–10 minutes before serving.
sausages standard 50g/2oz size	2 4 8	HIGH	Prick and place on a microwaveproof roasting rack in a dish if possible. Brush with a browning agent if liked or cook in a preheated browning dish. Microwave for 2½ minutes for 2; 4 minutes for 4; and 5 minutes for 8 sausages, turning over once halfway through the cooking time. Leave to stand for 2 minutes before serving.

VEAL

roast joint	per 450g/1lb	HIGH *or* MEDIUM	Place the joint on a microwaveproof rack or upturned saucer in a dish. Times are given for cooking on HIGH or MEDIUM. Both methods work well, but the latter is ideal for less-tender cuts or large joints. Calculate the cooking time according to weight and microwave for: *per 450g/1lb* HIGH 8½–9 minutes *or* MEDIUM 11–12 minutes Turn the joint over halfway through the cooking time. Cover with foil after cooking and leave to stand for 15–20 minutes before carving.

Beef and Mushroom Burgers.

Cooking Vegetables

ARTICHOKES

globe	1 2 4	HIGH	Discard the tough, outer leaves. Snip the tops off the remaining leaves and trim the stems to the base. Wash and stand upright in a microwaveproof bowl. Pour over the water and lemon juice for 90ml/6 tbsp water and 7.5ml/1½ tsp lemon juice for 1; 120ml/4fl oz/½ cup water and 15ml/1 tbsp lemon juice for 2; and 150ml/¼ pint/⅔ cup water and 30ml/2 tbsp lemon juice for 4. Cover and microwave for 5–6 minutes for 1; 10–11 minutes for 2; and 15–18 minutes for 4, basting and rearranging twice. Leave to stand for 5 minutes before serving.
Jerusalem	450g/1lb	HIGH	Peel and cut into even-size pieces. Place in a microwaveproof bowl with 60ml/4 tbsp water or 25g/1oz/2 tbsp butter. Cover and microwave for 8–10 minutes, stirring once. Leave to stand, covered, for 3–5 minutes before serving.

ASPARAGUS

fresh whole spears	450g/1lb	HIGH	Prepare and arrange in a shallow microwaveproof dish with pointed tops to the centre. Add 120ml/4fl oz/½ cup water. Cover and microwave for 12–14 minutes, rearranging the spears half way through the time but still keeping the tips to the centre of the dish.
fresh cut spears	450g/1lb	HIGH	Prepare and place in a large shallow microwaveproof dish. Add 120ml/4fl oz/½ cup water. Cover and microwave for 9–11 minutes, rearranging once. Leave to stand, covered, for 5 minutes before serving.

AUBERGINES

fresh cubes	450g/1lb	HIGH	Cut unpeeled aubergine into 2cm/¾in cubes. Place in a microwaveproof bowl with 25g/1oz/2 tbsp butter. Cover and microwave for 7–10 minutes, stirring every 3 minutes. Leave to stand, covered, for 4 minutes. Season *after* cooking.
fresh whole	225g/8oz 2 x 225g/8oz	HIGH	Peel off stalks, rinse and dry. Brush with a little oil and prick. Place on kitchen paper and microwave for 3–4 minutes for 1 aubergine; 4–6 minutes for 2, turning over once. Leave to stand for 4 minutes. Scoop out flesh and use as required.

BEANS

fresh green	225g/8oz whole 450g/1lb whole 225g/8oz cut 450g/1lb cut	HIGH	Place whole or cut beans in a microwaveproof bowl and add 30ml/2 tbsp water. Cover and microwave for 8–10 minutes for 225g/8oz whole beans; 15–18 minutes for 450g/1lb whole beans; 7–9 minutes for 225g/8oz cut beans; and 12–15 minutes for 450g/1lb cut beans, stirring once. Leave to stand, covered, for 2–3 minutes before serving.
fresh baby green whole or French whole	225g/8oz 450g/1lb	HIGH	Place in a microwaveproof bowl with 30ml/2 tbsp water. Cover and microwave for 7–9 minutes for 225g/8oz; 12–15 minutes for 450g/1lb, stirring 3 times. Leave to stand, covered, for 2–3 minutes, before serving.
fresh sliced runner beans	225g/8oz 450g/1lb	HIGH	Place in a microwaveproof bowl with 30ml/2 tbsp water. Cover and microwave for 7–9 minutes for 225g/8oz; 12–15 minutes for 450g/1lb, stirring 3–4 times. Leave to stand, covered, for 2–3 minutes before serving.
fresh shelled broad beans	225g/8oz 450g/1lb	HIGH	Place in a microwaveproof bowl and add the water: 75ml/5 tbsp for 225g/8oz beans; and 120ml/4fl oz/½ cup for 450g/1lb beans. Cover and microwave for 5–7 minutes for 225g/8oz; 6–10 minutes for 450g/1lb, stirring once. Leave to stand, covered, for 2–3 minutes before serving.

BEETROOT

fresh	4 medium	HIGH	Wash the beetroot and pierce the skin with a fork but do not peel. Place in a shallow microwaveproof dish with 60ml/4 tbsp water. Cover loosely and microwave for 14–16 minutes, rearranging twice. Leave to stand, covered, for 5 minutes before removing skins to serve or use.

BROCCOLI

fresh spears	225g/8oz 450g/1lb	HIGH	Place spears in a large shallow microwaveproof dish with tender heads to centre of dish. Add 60ml/4 tbsp water. Cover and microwave for 4–5 minutes for 225g/8oz; 8–9 minutes for 450g/1lb, rotating the dish once. Leave to stand, covered, for 2–4 minutes before serving.
fresh pieces	225g/8oz 450g/1lb	HIGH	Cut into 2.5cm/1in pieces. Place in a microwaveproof bowl with 60ml/4 tbsp water. Cover and microwave for 4½–5 minutes for 225g/8oz; 8½–9½ minutes for 450g/1lb, stirring once. Leave to stand, covered, for 3–5 minutes before serving.

BRUSSELS SPROUTS

fresh	450g/1lb 900g/2lb	HIGH	Remove outer leaves, trim and cross-cut base. Place in a microwaveproof dish and add water: 60ml/4 tbsp for 450g/1lb; 120ml/4/fl oz/½ cup for 900g/2lb. Cover and microwave for 6–7 minutes for 450g/1lb; 12–14 minute for 900g/2lb, stirring once. Leave to stand, covered, for 3–5 minutes before serving.

CABBAGE

fresh	225g/8oz 450g/1lb	HIGH	Core and shred, and place in a large microwaveproof dish. Add water: 60ml/4 tbsp for 225g/8oz; 120ml/4/fl oz/½ cup for 450g/1lb. Cover and microwave for 7–9 minutes for 225g/8oz; 9–11 minutes for 450g/1lb, stirring once. Leave to stand, covered, for 2 minutes before serving.

CARROTS

fresh baby whole and sliced	450g/1lb whole 450g/1lb sliced	HIGH	Place in a microwaveproof dish with 60ml/4 tbsp water. Cover and microwave for 12–14 minutes for whole; 10–12 minutes for sliced. Leave to stand, covered, for 3–5 minutes before serving.

CAULIFLOWER

fresh whole	675g/1½lb	MEDIUM	Trim but leave whole, and place floret-side down in a microwaveproof dish with 250ml/8fl oz/1 cup water. Cover and microwave for 16–17 minutes, turning over once. Leave to stand for 3–5 minutes before serving.
fresh florets	225g/8oz 450g/1lb	HIGH	Place in a microwaveproof dish with water: 45ml/3 tbsp for 225g/8oz; 60ml/4 tbsp for 450g/1lb. Cover and microwave for 7–8 minutes for 225g/8oz; 10–12 minutes for 450g/1lb, stirring once. Leave to stand for 3 minutes before serving.

CELERY

fresh sliced	1 head (about 9 stalks)	HIGH	Slice into 5mm/¼in pieces and place in a shallow microwaveproof dish with 30ml/2 tbsp water and 25g/1oz/2 tbsp butter. Cover and microwave for 5–6 minutes, stirring once. Leave to stand, covered, for 3 minutes before serving.
fresh celery hearts	4 hearts	HIGH	Halve each celery heart lengthways and place in a shallow microwaveproof dish. Add 30ml/2 tbsp water and a knob of butter if liked. Cover and microwave for 4½–5 minutes, turning once. Leave to stand, covered, for 3 minutes before serving.

CHINESE CABBAGE

fresh	450g/1lb	HIGH	Slice and place in a large microwaveproof dish. Add 30–45ml/2–3 tbsp water. Cover and microwave for 6–8 minutes, stirring once. Leave to stand, covered, for 3–5 minutes. Season after cooking.

COURGETTES

fresh	225g/8oz 450g/1lb	HIGH	Top and tail, and slice thinly. Place in a microwaveproof dish with butter: 25g/1oz/2 tbsp for 225g/8oz; 40g/1½oz/3 tbsp for 450g/1lb. Cover loosely and microwave for 4–6½ minutes for 225g/8oz; 6–8 minutes for 450g/1lb, stirring once. Leave to stand, covered, for 2–3 minutes before serving.

CURLY KALE fresh	450g/1lb	HIGH	Remove the thick stalk and stems, then shred. Place in a microwaveproof bowl with 150ml/¼ pint/⅔ cup water. Cover and microwave for 15–17 minutes, stirring every 5 minutes. Leave to stand for 2 minutes before serving.
FENNEL fresh sliced	450g/1lb	HIGH	Place in a microwaveproof bowl with 45ml/3 tbsp water. Cover and microwave for 9–10 minutes, stirring once. Leave to stand, covered, for 2–3 minutes before serving.
KOHLRABI fresh sliced	450g/1lb 900g/2lb	HIGH	Trim away the root ends and stems, scrub and peel the bulb and cut into 5mm/¼in slices. Place in a microwaveproof bowl with water: 45ml/3 tbsp for 450g/1lb; and 75ml/5 tbsp for 900g/2lb. Cover and microwave for 5–6 minutes for 450g/1lb; 9–11 minutes for 900g/2lb, stirring twice. Leave to stand, covered, for 3–4 minutes. Drain to serve.
LEEKS fresh whole	450g/1lb 900g/2lb	HIGH	Trim and slice from the top of the white to the green leaves in 2–3 places. Wash thoroughly and place in a microwaveproof dish with water: 45ml/3 tbsp for 450g/1lb; and 75ml/5 tbsp for 900g/2lb. Cover and microwave for 3–5 minutes for 450g/1lb; 6–8 minutes for 900g/2lb, rearranging twice. Leave to stand, covered, for 3–5 minutes before serving.
fresh sliced	450g/1lb	HIGH	Place in a microwaveproof dish with 45ml/3 tbsp water. Cover and microwave for 8–10 minutes, stirring once. Leave to stand, covered, for 2–3 minutes before serving.
MANGETOUTS fresh	115g/4oz 225g/8oz	HIGH	Trim and place in a microwaveproof bowl with water: 15ml/1 tbsp for 115g/4oz; 30ml/2 tbsp for 225g/8oz. Cover and microwave for 3–4 minutes for 115g/4oz; and 4–5 minutes for 225g/8oz, stirring once. Leave to stand, covered, for 2 minutes before serving.
MARROW fresh	450g/1lb	HIGH	Peel, remove seeds and cut into small neat dice. Place in a microwaveproof dish without water. Cover loosely and microwave for 7–10 minutes, stirring once. Leave to stand, covered, for 2–3 minutes before serving.
MUSHROOMS fresh whole	225g/8oz 450g/1lb	HIGH	Trim and wipe mushrooms. Place in a microwaveproof dish with water or butter: 25g/1oz/2 tbsp butter or 30ml/2 tbsp water for 225g/8oz mushrooms; and 40g/1½oz/3 tbsp butter or 45ml/3 tbsp water for 450g/1lb mushrooms. Cover and microwave for 3–4 minutes for 225g/8oz; and 4–5 minutes for 450g/1lb, stirring twice. Leave to stand for 1–2 minutes before serving. Season after cooking.
fresh sliced	225g/8oz 450g/1lb	HIGH	As above but microwave for 2–3 minutes for 225g/8oz mushrooms; and 3–4 minutes for 450g/1lb mushrooms.
OKRA fresh	450g/1lb	HIGH	Top and tail, and sprinkle lightly with salt. Leave to drain for 30 minutes. Rinse and place in a microwaveproof dish with 30ml/2 tbsp water or 25g/1oz/2 tbsp butter. Cover and microwave for 8–10 minutes, stirring once. Leave to stand, covered, for 3 minutes before serving.
ONIONS fresh whole	450g/1lb or 4 medium	HIGH	Peel and place in a microwaveproof dish. Cover and microwave for 10–12 minutes, rearranging and rotating once. Leave to stand, covered, for 2 minutes before serving.
fresh sliced	450g/1lb	HIGH	Peel and cut into thin wedges or slices. Place in a microwaveproof dish with 25g/1oz/2 tbsp butter and 30ml/2 tbsp water. Cover loosely and microwave for 7–10 minutes, stirring once. Leave to stand, covered, for 5 minutes before serving.

PAK CHOI (or bok choy cabbage)	450g/1lb	HIGH	Slice stalks and leaves and place in a large microwaveproof dish. Add 30ml/2 tbsp water and microwave for 6–8 minutes, stirring once. Leave to stand for 3–5 minutes before serving.
PARSNIPS fresh whole	450g/1lb	HIGH	Peel and prick with a fork. Arrange in a microwaveproof dish with tapered ends to the centre. Dot with 15g/½oz/1 tbsp butter and add 45ml/3 tbsp water and 15ml/1 tbsp lemon juice. Cover and microwave for 9–12 minutes, rearranging once. Leave to stand, covered, for 3 minutes before serving.
fresh slices	450g/1lb	HIGH	Peel and slice. Place in a microwaveproof dish with 15g/½oz/1 tbsp butter, 45ml/3 tbsp water and 15ml/1 tbsp lemon juice. Cover and microwave for 9–12 minutes, stirring twice. Leave to stand, covered, for 3 minutes before serving.
PEAS fresh	115g/4oz 225g/8oz 450g/1lb	HIGH	Place shelled peas in a microwaveproof bowl with butter and water: 15g/½oz/1 tbsp butter and 10ml/2 tsp water for 115g/4oz peas; 25g/1oz/2 tbsp butter and 15ml/1 tbsp water for 225g/8oz peas; and 50g/2oz/4 tbsp butter and 30ml/2 tbsp water for 450g/1lb peas. Cover and microwave for 3 minutes for 115g/4oz; 4–5 minutes for 225g/8oz; and 6–8 minutes for 450g/1lb, stirring once. Leave to stand, covered, for 3–5 minutes before serving.
POTATOES mashed or creamed	900g/2lb	HIGH	Peel and cut into 1.5cm/½in cubes. Place in a microwaveproof bowl with 75ml/5 tbsp water. Cover and microwave for 11–13 minutes, stirring once. Leave to stand, covered, for 5 minutes. Drain and mash with butter and seasoning to taste.
new potatoes or old, peeled and quartered	450g/1lb	HIGH	Scrub and scrape new potatoes if liked. Peel and quarter old potatoes. Place in a microwaveproof dish with 60ml/4 tbsp water. Cover and microwave for 7–10 minutes for new; and 6–8 minutes for old, stirring once. Leave to stand, covered, for 5 minutes before serving.
jacket baked	175g/6oz 2 x 175g/6oz 3 x 175g/6oz 4 x 175g/6oz	HIGH	Scrub and prick the skin. Place on a double sheet of absorbent kitchen paper. Microwave for 4–6 minutes for 1; 6–8 minutes for 2; 8–12 minutes for 3; 12–15 minutes for 4, turning over once. If cooking more than 2 potatoes, arrange in a ring pattern. Leave to stand for 5 minutes, before serving.
PUMPKIN fresh	450g/1lb	HIGH	Remove the skin, seeds and membrane and cut into 2.5cm/1in cubes. Place in a microwaveproof dish with 15g/½oz/1 tbsp butter. Cover and microwave for 4–6 minutes, stirring twice. Leave to stand for 3 minutes, then season to serve plain, or mash with cream and herbs.
SPINACH fresh	450g/1lb	HIGH	Chop or shred and rinse. Place in a microwaveproof bowl without any extra water. Cover and microwave for 6–8 minutes, stirring once. Leave to stand for 2 minutes before serving. Season after cooking.
SQUASH fresh	450g/1lb	HIGH	Pierce whole squash with a knife several times. Microwave for 3–5 minutes per 450g/1lb until the flesh pierces easily with a skewer. Leave to stand for 5 minutes. Halve, scoop out the seeds and fibres and discard. Serve fresh in chunks or mash with butter.
SWEDES fresh	450g/1lb	HIGH	Peel and cut into 1cm/½in cubes. Place in a microwaveproof bowl with 15g/½oz/1 tbsp butter and 30ml/2 tbsp water. Cover and microwave for 10–12 minutes, stirring twice. Leave to stand, covered, for 4 minutes. Drain to serve.

SWEETCORN

corn on the cob, fresh husked	1 x 175g/6oz 2 x 175g/6oz 3 x 175g/6oz 4 x 175g/6oz	HIGH	Wrap individually in clear film or place in a microwaveproof dish with 60ml/4 tbsp water and cover. Place or arrange evenly in the oven and microwave for 3–4 minutes for 1; 5–6 minutes for 2; 7–8 minutes for 3; and 9–10 minutes for 4, rotating and rearranging once. Leave to stand, covered, for 3–5 minutes before serving.

SWEET POTATOES

fresh	450g/1lb, whole 450g/1lb, cubed	HIGH	If cooking whole, prick the skins and place on absorbent kitchen paper. Microwave for 7–9 minutes, turning twice. Allow to cool for handling and peel away the skins to serve. To cook cubes, place in a microwaveproof bowl with 45ml/3 tbsp water. Cover and microwave for 6–8 minutes, stirring twice. Drain and toss with butter and seasoning. Leave to stand for 2 minutes before serving.

SWISS CHARD

fresh	450g/1lb	HIGH	Remove and discard the thick stalk and shred the leaves. Place in a microwaveproof dish with 150ml/¼ pint/⅔ cup water. Cover and microwave for 5½–6½ minutes, stirring every 3 minutes. Leave to stand for 2 minutes before serving. Season after cooking.

TOMATOES

whole and halves	1 medium 4 medium 4 large (beef)	HIGH	Prick whole and/or halved tomatoes, arrange in a circle on a plate, cut-sides up. Dot with butter and season to taste. Microwave for ½ minute for 1 medium; 2–2½ minutes for 4 medium; and 3½–4 minutes for 4 large (beef) tomatoes, according to size and ripeness. Leave to stand for 1–2 minutes before serving.

TURNIPS

whole	450g/1lb	HIGH	Choose only small to medium turnips. Peel and prick with a fork. Arrange in a ring pattern in a shallow microwaveproof dish. Dot with 15g/½oz/1 tbsp butter and add 45ml/3 tbsp water. Cover and microwave for 14–16 minutes, rearranging once. Leave to stand, covered, for 3 minutes before serving.
sliced or cubed	450g/1lb	HIGH	Place slices or cubes in a microwaveproof dish with 15g/½oz/1 tbsp butter and 45ml/3 tbsp water. Cover and microwave for 11–12 minutes for slices; and 12–14 minutes for cubes. Leave to stand, covered, for 3 minutes before serving.

Broccoli and Chestnut Terrine.

Middle-Eastern Vegetable Stew.

Cooking Frozen Vegetables

ASPARAGUS
frozen whole spears — 450g/1lb — HIGH — Place in a microwaveproof dish with 120ml/4fl oz/½ cup water. Cover and microwave for 9–12 minutes, rearranging once. Leave to stand for 5 minutes before serving.

BEANS
frozen green beans — 225g/8oz whole / 450g/1lb whole / 225g/8oz cut / 450g/1lb cut — HIGH — Place in a microwaveproof bowl with water, cover and microwave with 30ml/2tbsp water for 9–10 minutes for 225g/8oz whole beans; 60ml/4 tbsp water and 14–15 minutes for 450g/1lb whole beans; 30ml/2 tbsp water and 6–7 minutes for 225g/8oz cut beans; and 60ml/4 tbsp water and 10–12 minutes for 450g/1lb cut beans, stirring once. Leave to stand, covered, for 2–3 minutes before serving.

frozen baby green or French whole beans — 225g/8oz / 450g/1lb — HIGH — Place in a microwaveproof bowl with water, cover and microwave with 30ml/2 tbsp water for 8–9 minutes for 225g/8oz beans; and 60ml/4 tbsp water and 13–15 minutes for 450g/1lb beans, stirring 3 times. Leave to stand, covered, for 2–3 minutes before serving.

frozen sliced runner beans — 225g/8oz / 450g/1lb — HIGH — Place in a microwaveproof bowl with water, cover and microwave with 30ml/2 tbsp water for 6–7 minutes for 225g/8oz beans; and 60ml/4 tbsp water and 10–12 minutes for 450g/1lb beans, stirring twice. Leave to stand, covered, for 2–3 minutes before serving.

frozen shelled broad beans — 225g/8oz / 450g/1lb — HIGH — Place in a microwaveproof bowl with water, cover and microwave with 60ml/4 tbsp water for 6–7 minutes for 225g/8oz beans; and 120ml/4½fl oz/½ cup and 10–11 minutes for 450g/1lb beans, stirring twice. Leave to stand, covered, for 2–3 minutes before serving.

BROCCOLI
frozen spears — 450g/1lb — HIGH — Place in a microwaveproof dish with 60ml/4 tbsp water. Cover and microwave for 13–14 minutes, stirring once. Leave to stand, covered, for 2–3 minutes before serving.

BRUSSELS SPROUTS
frozen — 450g/1lb — HIGH — Place in a microwaveproof dish with 30ml/2 tbsp water. Cover and microwave for 10–11 minutes, stirring once. Leave to stand, covered, for 3–5 minutes before serving.

CABBAGE
frozen — 225g/8oz / 450g/1lb — HIGH — Place in a large microwaveproof dish with water, cover and microwave with 60ml/4 tbsp water for 6–8 minutes for 225g/8oz; and 120ml/4½fl oz/½ cup water and 8–10 minutes for 450g/1lb, stirring once. Leave to stand, covered, for 2 minutes before serving.

CARROTS
frozen whole and sliced — 450g/1lb whole / 450g/1lb sliced — HIGH — Place in a microwaveproof dish with water. Cover and microwave with 30ml/2 tbsp water for 10–12 minutes for whole carrots; and 30ml/2 tbsp water and 8–10 minutes for sliced carrots, stirring once. Leave to stand, covered, for 2–3 minutes before serving.

CAULIFLOWER
frozen florets — 450g/1lb — HIGH — Place in a microwaveproof dish with 60ml/4 tbsp water. Cover and microwave for 8–9 minutes, stirring once. Leave to stand, covered, for 2–3 minutes before serving.

COURGETTES
frozen sliced — 450g/1lb — HIGH — Place in a shallow microwaveproof dish with 40g/1½oz/3 tbsp butter if liked. Cover loosely and microwave for 7–8 minutes, stirring once. Leave to stand, covered, for 2–3 minutes before serving.

LEEKS
frozen sliced | 450g/1lb | HIGH | Place in a microwaveproof dish with 45ml/3 tbsp water. Cover and microwave for 11–12 minutes, stirring once. Leave to stand, covered, for 2–3 minutes before serving.

MANGETOUTS
frozen | 225g/8oz | HIGH | Place in a microwaveproof dish with 30ml/2 tbsp water. Cover and microwave for 3–4 minutes, stirring once. Leave to stand, covered, for 2–3 minutes before serving.

MIXED VEGETABLES
frozen | 225g/8oz 450g/1lb | HIGH | Place in a microwaveproof dish with water. Cover and microwave with 30ml/2 tbsp water for 4–5 minutes for 225g/8oz; and 30ml/2 tbsp water and 7–8 minutes for 450g/1lb, stirring once. Leave to stand, covered, for 2 minutes before serving.

MUSHROOMS
frozen whole button | 115g/4oz 225g/8oz | HIGH | Place in a shallow microwaveproof dish with a knob of butter. Cover and microwave for 3–4 minutes for 115g/4oz; and 5–6 minutes for 225g/8oz, stirring twice. Leave to stand, covered, for 1–2 minutes. Season to taste to serve.

PARSNIPS
frozen whole | 450g/1lb | HIGH | Arrange in a shallow microwaveproof dish with tapered ends to centre. Cover and microwave for 9–10 minutes, rearranging once. Toss in butter and seasonings to serve. Leave to stand, covered, for 2–3 minutes before serving.

PEAS
frozen | 225g/8oz 450g/1lb | HIGH | Place in a microwaveproof dish with water. Cover and microwave with 30ml/2 tbsp water for 4–6 minutes for 225g/8oz; and 60ml/4 tbsp water and 6–8 minutes for 450g/1lb, stirring once. Leave to stand, covered, for 3 minutes.

SPINACH
frozen | 275g/10oz packet | HIGH | Place in a microwaveproof dish. Cover and microwave for 7–9 minutes, stirring twice to break up during cooking. Season *after* cooking.

SWEDES
frozen cubed swede | 450g/1lb | HIGH | Place in a microwaveproof dish, cover and microwave for 8–10 minutes, stirring twice. Leave to stand, covered, for 2–3 minutes. Toss in butter and seasonings or mash with same to a purée.

SWEETCORN
frozen sweetcorn kernels | 450g/1lb | HIGH | Place in a microwaveproof dish with 60ml/4 tbsp water. Cover and microwave for 7–8 minutes, stirring once. Leave to stand, covered, for 2–3 minutes before serving.

Summer Vegetable Braise.

Mixed Mushroom Ragout.

Cooking Pasta, Pulses and Grains

BARLEY pot barley	175g/6oz	HIGH *then* MEDIUM	Toast if liked before cooking. Place in a microwaveproof dish with 1 litre/ 1¾ pints/4 cups boiling water and a pinch of salt if liked. Cover loosely and microwave on HIGH for 3 minutes, then on MEDIUM for 40 minutes. Leave to stand for 5–10 minutes before fluffing with a fork to serve.
BULGUR grains	225g/8oz	HIGH *then* MEDIUM	Place in a microwaveproof dish with 550ml/18fl oz/2¼ cups boiling water and a pinch of salt if liked. Cover loosely and microwave on HIGH for 3 minutes, then on MEDIUM for 9–12 minutes. Leave to stand for 5–10 minutes before fluffing with a fork to serve.
COUSCOUS pre-cooked	350g/12oz	MEDIUM	Place in a microwaveproof dish with 250ml/8fl oz/1 cup boiling water and 50g/2oz/4 tbsp butter. Cover loosely and microwave for 15 minutes. Leave to stand for 5–10 minutes before fluffing with a fork to serve.
DRIED BEANS aduki black black-eyed borlotti broad butter cannellini flageolet haricot mung pinto red kidney soya	225g/8oz	HIGH *then* MEDIUM	Soak dried beans overnight in cold water or hasten soaking by par-cooking in the microwave. Place the dried beans in a microwaveproof bowl with boiling water to cover. Cover and microwave on HIGH for 5 minutes. Leave to stand, covered, for 1½ hours before draining to cook. Place soaked or par-cooked beans in a microwaveproof dish and cover with boiling water. Cover and microwave all beans on HIGH for 10 minutes. Reduce the power to MEDIUM and microwave aduki, black-eyed, mung and pinto beans for 10–15 minutes; and black, borlotti, broad, butter, cannellini, flageolet, haricot, red kidney and soya beans for 20–25 minutes, adding extra boiling water to cover if needed. Drain to use.
DRIED CHICK- PEAS	225g/8oz	HIGH *then* MEDIUM	Soak dried peas overnight or according to packet instructions. Place soaked peas in a microwaveproof dish and cover with boiling water. Cover and microwave on HIGH for 10 minutes, then on MEDIUM for 20–25 minutes, adding extra boiling water to cover if needed. Drain to use.
DRIED WHOLE GREEN PEAS	225g/8oz	HIGH *then* MEDIUM	Soak dried peas overnight or according to packet instructions. Place soaked peas in a microwaveproof dish and cover with boiling water. Cover and microwave on HIGH for 10 minutes, then on MEDIUM for 10–15 minutes, adding extra boiling water to cover if needed. Drain to use.
DRIED SPLIT PEAS	225g/8oz	HIGH	Soak dried peas overnight or according to packet instructions. Place soaked peas in a microwaveproof dish and cover with boiling water. Cover and microwave on HIGH for 10 minutes. Drain to use.
DRIED LENTILS	225g/8oz	HIGH	Place the lentils in a microwaveproof dish with a few seasoning vegetables such as chopped onion, celery, carrot or bouquet garni and a squeeze of lemon juice. Add 900ml/1½ pints/3¾ cups boiling water or stock. Cover and microwave for 15–25 minutes, stirring once halfway through cooking. Cook for the shorter length of time if the lentils are to be served in a salad mixture or as a meal accompaniment, the longer time if the lentils are to be puréed for use.
MILLET	225g/8oz	HIGH *then* MEDIUM	Toast if liked before cooking. Place in a microwaveproof dish with 650ml/ 22fl oz/2¾ cups boiling water and a pinch of salt if liked. Cover loosely and microwave on HIGH for 3 minutes, then on MEDIUM for 12 minutes. Leave to stand for 5–10 minutes before fluffing with a fork to serve.

OATS grains	175g/6oz	HIGH *then* MEDIUM	Toast if liked before cooking. Place in a microwaveproof dish with 750ml/ 1¼ pints/3 cups boiling water and a pinch of salt if liked. Cover loosely and microwave on HIGH for 3 minutes, then on MEDIUM for 20–22 minutes. Leave to stand for 5–10 minutes before fluffing with a fork to serve.
PASTA fresh: egg noodles spaghetti tagliatelle ravioli	225g/8oz	HIGH	Place the pasta in a large microwaveproof dish. Cover with 750ml/ 1¼ pints/3 cups boiling water and add 5ml/1 tsp oil. Cover loosely and microwave for 2–2½ minutes for egg noodles; 4–6 minutes for spaghetti; 2–3 minutes for tagliatelle; and 6–8 minutes for ravioli, stirring once halfway through the cooking time. Leave to stand for 2 minutes before draining to serve.
dried: egg noodles spaghetti tagliatelle short-cut macaroni pasta shapes ravioli	225g/8oz	HIGH	Place the pasta in a large microwaveproof dish. Add a generous 1.2 litres/ 2 pints/5 cups of boiling water and 5ml/1 tsp oil. Cover loosely and microwave: 6 minutes for egg noodles; 10–12 minutes for spaghetti; 6 minutes for tagliatelle; 10 minutes for short-cut macaroni; 10-12 minutes for pasta shapes; and 10 minutes for ravioli, stirring once halfway through the cooking time. Leave to stand for 3–5 minutes before draining to use.
RICE long grain white	115g/4oz 225g/8oz	HIGH *then* MEDIUM	Place the rice in a large microwaveproof dish. Add boiling water: 300ml/ ½ pint/1¼ cups for 115g/4oz rice; and 550ml/18fl oz/2¼ cups for 225g/8oz rice with a pinch of salt and knob of butter if liked. Cover loosely and microwave on HIGH for 3 minutes. Stir well then re-cover and microwave on MEDIUM for 12 minutes. Leave to stand, covered, for 5 minutes before fluffing with a fork to serve.
long grain brown	115g/4oz 225g/8oz	HIGH *then* MEDIUM	Place the rice in a large microwaveproof dish. Add boiling water: 300ml/ ½ pint/1¼ cups for 115g/4oz; 550ml/18fl oz/2¼ cups for 225g/8oz rice with a pinch of salt and knob of butter if liked. Cover loosely and microwave on HIGH for 3 minutes. Stir well then re-cover and microwave on MEDIUM for 25 minutes. Leave to stand, covered, for 5 minutes before fluffing with a fork to serve.
long grain and wild rice mix	400g/14oz packet	HIGH *then* MEDIUM	Place the rice mix in a microwaveproof dish with 650ml/22fl oz/2¾ cups boiling water, a pinch of salt and knob of butter if liked. Cover loosely and microwave on HIGH for 3 minutes. Stir well, re-cover and microwave on MEDIUM for 12 minutes, stirring once. Leave to stand, covered, for 5 minutes before fluffing with a fork to serve.
RYE grains	175g/6oz	HIGH *then* MEDIUM	Soak the rye grains for 6–8 hours in cold water then drain. Place in a microwaveproof dish with 750ml/1¼ pints/3 cups boiling water. Cover loosely and microwave on HIGH for 3 minutes, then on MEDIUM for 40 minutes. Leave to stand 5–10 minutes before fluffing with a fork to serve.
WHEAT grains	175g/6oz	HIGH *then* MEDIUM	Soak wheat grains for 6–8 hours in cold water then drain. Place in a microwaveproof dish with 1 litre/1¾ pints/4 cups boiling water. Cover loosely and microwave on HIGH for 3 minutes, then on MEDIUM for 40 minutes. Leave to stand 5–10 minutes before fluffing with a fork to serve.

Cooking Fruit

APPLES poached in light syrup	450g/1lb	HIGH	Peel, core and slice apples and place in a microwaveproof bowl with 300ml/½ pint/1¼ cups hot sugar syrup. Cover loosely and microwave for 3 minutes, stirring once. Leave to stand, covered, for 5 minutes.
	900g/2lb	HIGH	As above, but microwave for 5–6 minutes.
stewed	450g/1lb	HIGH	Peel, core and slice apples and place in a microwaveproof bowl with 115g/4oz/½ cup sugar. Cover loosely and microwave for 6–8 minutes, stirring once. Leave to stand, covered, for 2–3 minutes.
baked	4 large	HIGH	Wash and remove cores from the apples and score around the middle to prevent bursting. Place in a microwaveproof dish, stuff with a little dried fruit if liked. Pour 120ml/4fl oz/½ cup water around fruit and microwave for 9–10 minutes, rearranging once. Leave to stand, covered, for 3–4 minutes before serving.
APRICOTS poached in light syrup	6–8	HIGH	Skin, halve and stone, slicing if preferred. Place in a microwaveproof bowl with 300ml/½ pint/1¼ cups hot sugar syrup. Cover loosely and microwave for 3–4 minutes, stirring once. Leave to stand, covered, for 5 minutes.
stewed	6–8	HIGH	Stone and wash. Place in a microwaveproof bowl, sprinkle with 115g/4oz/½ cup sugar. Cover and microwave for 6–8 minutes, stirring once. Leave to stand, covered, for 5 minutes before serving.
BANANAS baked	2 large	HIGH	Peel and halve the bananas lengthways. Place in a microwaveproof dish with a little sugar and fruit juice. Microwave for 3–4 minutes, stirring or rearranging twice.
BLACKBERRIES poached in light syrup	450g/1lb	HIGH	Hull and rinse. Place in a microwaveproof bowl with 300ml/½ pint/1¼ cups hot sugar syrup. Cover loosely and microwave for 2 minutes, stirring once. Leave to stand, covered, for 5 minutes.
BLACKCURRANTS fresh	450g/1lb	HIGH	Top and tail and place in a microwaveproof dish with 115g/4oz/½ cup sugar and 30ml/2 tbsp water. Cover loosely and microwave for 5 minutes, stirring once. Leave to stand, covered, for 5 minutes.
CHERRIES poached in light syrup	450g/1lb	HIGH	Prick and stone if preferred. Place in a microwaveproof bowl with 300ml/½ pint/1¼ cups of hot sugar syrup. Cover loosely and microwave for 2–3 minutes, stirring once. Leave to stand, covered, for 5 minutes.
stewed	450g/1lb	HIGH	Stone, wash and place in a microwaveproof bowl with 115g/4oz/½ cup sugar and a little grated lemon rind if liked. Cover and microwave for 4–5 minutes, stirring once. Leave to stand, covered, for 3–5 minutes.
CRANBERRIES cranberry sauce	450g/1lb	HIGH	Place the cranberries, 90ml/6 tbsp water and 350g/12oz/1¾ cups sugar in a large microwaveproof bowl. Cover with vented cling film and microwave for 18–20 minutes, stirring every 6 minutes, until pulpy.
DAMSONS poached in light syrup	450g/1lb, whole or halved	HIGH	Prick whole damsons or halve and stone if preferred. Place in a microwaveproof bowl with 300ml/½ pint/1¼ cups hot sugar syrup. Cover loosely and microwave for 3 minutes for whole damsons; 2 minutes for halves, stirring once. Leave to stand, covered, for 5 minutes.

stewed	450g/1lb	HIGH	Stone and wash. Place in a microwaveproof bowl with 115g/4oz/½ cup sugar and a little grated lemon rind if liked. Cover and microwave for 4–5 minutes, stirring once. Leave to stand, covered, for 3–5 minutes.
GOOSEBERRIES fresh	450g/1lb	HIGH	Top and tail and place in a microwaveproof bowl with 30ml/2 tbsp water. Cover and microwave for 4–6 minutes. Stir in 115g/4oz/½ cup sugar and leave to stand, covered, for 5 minutes.
GREENGAGES poached in light syrup	450g/1lb whole or halved	HIGH	Prick whole greengages or halve and stone if preferred. Place in a microwaveproof bowl with 300ml/½ pint/1¼ cups hot sugar syrup. Cover loosely and microwave for 3 minutes for whole greengages; 2 minutes for halves, stirring once. Leave to stand, covered, for 5 minutes.
stewed	450g/1lb		Stone and wash. Place in a microwaveproof bowl with 115g/4oz/½ cup sugar and a little grated lemon rind if liked. Cover and microwave for 4–5 minutes, stirring once. Leave to stand, covered, for 3–5 minutes.
NECTARINES poached in light syrup	8	HIGH	Skin and prick thoroughly. Place in a microwaveproof bowl with 300ml/½ pint/1¼ cups hot sugar syrup and a dash of lemon juice. Cover loosely and microwave for 6 minutes, stirring once. Leave to stand, covered, for 5 minutes.
stewed	4 medium	HIGH	Stone, wash and slice. Place in a microwaveproof bowl with 115g/4oz/½ cup sugar. Cover and microwave for 4–5 minutes, stirring once. Leave to stand, covered, for 5 minutes.
ORANGES poached in light syrup	4	HIGH	Peel if preferred, or scrub the skin, then finely slice. Place in a microwaveproof bowl with 300ml/½ pint/1¼ cups hot sugar syrup. Cover loosely and microwave for 3 minutes, stirring once. Leave to stand, covered, for 5 minutes.
PEACHES poached in light syrup	4 whole or sliced	HIGH	Skin and prick thoroughly or skin, stone and slice. Place in a microwaveproof bowl with 300ml/½ pint/1¼ cups hot sugar syrup. Cover loosely and microwave for 4 minutes for whole peaches; 3 minutes for slices, stirring once. Leave to stand, covered, for 5 minutes.
stewed	4 medium	HIGH	Stone, wash and slice. Place in a microwaveproof bowl with 115g/4oz/½ cup sugar. Cover and microwave for 4–5 minutes, stirring once. Leave to stand, covered, for 5 minutes.
PEARS poached in light syrup	900g/2lb whole dessert 900g/2lb whole cooking 900g/2lb halved dessert	HIGH	Peel and prick if kept whole, or halve and core. Place in a microwaveproof bowl with 300ml/½ pint/1¼ cups hot sugar syrup. Cover loosely and microwave for 5 minutes for whole dessert pears; 10 minutes for whole cooking pears: and 3 minutes for halved dessert pears, stirring once. Leave to stand, covered, for 5 minutes.
stewed	6 medium	HIGH	Peel, halve and core. Dissolve 75g/3oz/⅓ cup sugar in a little water and pour over the pears. Cover loosely and microwave for 8–10 minutes, stirring once. Leave to stand, covered, for 5 minutes.
PINEAPPLE poached in light syrup	900g/2lb	HIGH	Peel, core and cut into bite-size pieces. Place in a microwaveproof bowl with 300ml/½ pint/1¼ cups hot sugar syrup. Cover loosely and microwave for 5 minutes, stirring once. Leave to stand, covered, for 5 minutes.

PLUMS
poached in light syrup | 450g/1lb whole or halved | HIGH | Prick if kept whole or halve and stone. Place in a microwaveproof bowl with 300ml/½ pint/1¼ cups hot sugar syrup. Cover loosely and microwave for 3 minutes for whole plums; 2 minutes for halved, stirring once. Leave to stand, covered, for 5 minutes.

stewed | 450g/1lb | HIGH | Stone and wash. Place in a microwaveproof bowl with 115g/4oz/½ cup sugar and a little grated lemon rind if liked. Cover and microwave for 4–5 minutes, stirring once. Leave to stand, covered, for 3–5 minutes.

RASPBERRIES
poached in light syrup | 450g/1lb | HIGH | Hull and rinse. Place in a microwaveproof bowl with 300ml/½ pint/1¼ cups hot sugar syrup. Cover loosely and microwave for 2 minutes, stirring once. Leave to stand, covered, for 5 minutes.

REDCURRANTS
fresh | 450g/1lb | HIGH | Top and tail and place in a microwaveproof bowl with 115g/4oz/½ cup sugar and 30ml/2 tbsp water. Cover loosely and microwave for 5 minutes, stirring once. Leave to stand for 5 minutes.

RHUBARB
fresh | 350g/12oz | HIGH | Cut into 2.5cm/1in lengths. Place in a microwaveproof bowl with 30ml/2 tbsp water. Cover loosely and microwave for 6–7 minutes, stirring once. Stir in 115g/4oz/½ cup sugar and 5ml/1 tsp lemon juice. Leave to stand, covered, for 2–3 minutes.

poached in light syrup | 450g/1lb | HIGH | Cut into 2.5cm/1in lengths. Place in a microwaveproof bowl with 300ml/½ pint/1¼ cups hot sugar syrup. Cover loosely and microwave for 4 minutes, stirring once. Leave to stand, covered, for 5 minutes.

STRAWBERRIES
poached in light syrup | 450g/1lb | HIGH | Hull and rinse. Place in a microwaveproof bowl with 300ml/½ pint/1¼ cups hot sugar syrup. Cover loosely and microwave for 2 minutes, stirring once. Leave to stand, covered, for 5 minutes.

SUGAR SYRUP
To make sugar syrup for poaching fruits: place 115g/4oz/½ cup sugar and 300ml/½ pint/1¼ cups water in a microwaveproof jug. Microwave on HIGH for 4–5 minutes, stirring 3 times. Use as required. Makes 300ml/½ pint/1¼ cups.

Plum and Walnut Crumble.

Baked Apples with Apricots.

Defrosting Fish and Shellfish

COD

frozen steaks	1 x 225g/8oz 2 x 225g/8oz 4 x 225g/8oz	DEFROST	To defrost, place in a microwaveproof dish, cover and microwave for 2–2 ½ minutes for 1 steak; 3–4 minutes for 2 steaks; and 6–7 minutes for 4 steaks, turning over or rearranging once. Leave to stand, covered, for 10 minutes before using.
frozen fillets	450g/1lb	DEFROST	To defrost, place in a microwaveproof dish with the thicker portions to the outer edge. Cover and microwave for 7–8 minutes, rearranging once. Leave to stand for 5 minutes before using.

CRABMEAT

frozen	225g/8oz	DEFROST	Leave in wrappings. Microwave for 4 minutes, turning over once. Leave to stand for 2 minutes, then flake to use.

FISHCAKES

frozen	4 x 75g/3oz	DEFROST	To defrost, unwrap and place in a shallow microwaveproof dish. Cover and microwave for 5–6½ minutes, rearranging once. Leave to stand for 2 minutes before cooking.

HADDOCK

frozen steaks	1 x 225g/8oz 2 x 225g/8oz 4 x 225g/8oz	DEFROST	To defrost, place in a microwaveproof dish, cover and microwave for 2–2½ minutes for 1 steak; 3–4 minutes for 2 steaks; and 6–7 minutes for 4 steaks, turning over or rearranging once. Leave to stand for 10 minutes before using.
frozen fillets	450g/1lb	DEFROST	To defrost, place in a microwaveproof dish with the thicker portions to the outer edge. Cover and microwave for 7–8 minutes, rearranging once. Leave to stand for 5 minutes before using.

HALIBUT

frozen steaks	1 x 225g/8oz 2 x 225g/8oz 4 x 225g/8oz	DEFROST	To defrost, place in a microwaveproof dish, cover and microwave for 2–2½ minutes for 1 steak; 3–4 minutes for 2 steaks; and 6–7 minutes for 4 steaks, turning over or rearranging once. Leave to stand for 10 minutes before using.

HERRING

frozen whole	per 450g/1lb	DEFROST	To defrost, place in a shallow microwaveproof dish and microwave for 5–7 minutes per 450g/1lb, turning over once. Leave to stand for 10 minutes before using.

KIPPERS

frozen fillets	175g/6oz boil-in-the-bag	HIGH	To defrost *and* cook, place the frozen boil-in-the-bag on a plate and snip a couple of vents in the bag. Microwave for 5–6 minutes, turning over once. Leave to stand for 2–3 minutes before serving.

LOBSTER

frozen whole cooked	per 450g/1lb	DEFROST	To defrost, place in a microwaveproof dish, cover and microwave for 12–15 minutes per 450g/1lb, giving the dish a quarter turn every 2 minutes and turning over after 6 minutes. Leave to stand for 5 minutes before serving.

MACKEREL

frozen whole	per 450g/1lb	DEFROST	To defrost, place in a shallow microwaveproof dish and microwave for 5–7 minutes per 450g/1lb, turning over once. Leave to stand for 10 minutes before using.

MUSSELS

frozen cooked shelled	225g/8oz	DEFROST	To defrost, spread the mussels out on a plate in a single layer. Microwave for 3½–4 minutes, stirring to rearrange once. Leave to stand for 2 minutes before using.

PLAICE

frozen fillets	450g/1lb	DEFROST	To defrost, place in a microwaveproof dish with the thicker portions to the outer edge. Cover and microwave for 7–8 minutes, rearranging once. Leave to stand for 5 minutes before using.

frozen whole	1 x 275g/10oz 2 x 275g/10oz	DEFROST	To defrost, place on a plate, cover and microwave for 4–6 minutes for 1 plaice; and 10–12 minutes for 2 plaice, shielding the tail end with a little foil halfway through cooking if necessary. Leave to stand for 5 minutes before using.

PRAWNS AND SHRIMPS

frozen cooked	450g/1lb	DEFROST	To defrost, place in a microwaveproof dish and microwave for 7–8 minutes, stirring twice. Leave to stand for 2–3 minutes before using.

RED OR GREY MULLET

frozen whole	2 x 200–250g/7–9oz 4 x 200–250g/7–9oz	DEFROST	To defrost, place in a shallow microwaveproof dish and microwave for 9–11 minutes for 2 whole fish; and 19–21 minutes for 4 whole fish, turning or rearranging twice. Leave to stand for 5 minutes before using.

RED SNAPPER

frozen whole	450–550g/1–1¼lb	MEDIUM	To defrost individually (for best results), place in a shallow microwaveproof dish, cover and microwave for 2½–3½ minutes, turning over once. Rinse in cold water then pat dry. Leave to stand for 2–3 minutes before using.

SALMON AND SALMON TROUT

frozen steaks	2 x 225g/8oz 4 x 225g/8oz 4 x 175g/6oz	DEFROST	To defrost, place in a shallow microwaveproof dish, cover and microwave for 4–5 minutes for 2 x 225g/8oz steaks; 10–12 minutes for 4 x 225g/8oz steaks; and 10 minutes for 4 x 175g/6oz steaks, turning over and rearranging once. Leave to stand, covered, for 5–10 minutes before using.
frozen whole salmon or salmon trout	450g/1lb 900g/2lb 1.5kg/3–3½lb 1.75kg/4–4½lb	DEFROST	To defrost, place in a shallow microwaveproof dish, cover and microwave for 6–8 minutes for a 450g/1lb fish; 12–16 minutes for a 900g/2lb fish; 18–20 minutes for a 1.5kg/3–3½lb fish; and 22–24 minutes for a 1.75kg/4–4½lb fish, turning over and rotating the dish twice. Shield the head and tail with a little foil as necessary. Leave to stand, covered, for 5–10 minutes before using.

SCALLOPS

frozen	350g/12oz packet 450g/1lb	DEFROST	To defrost, place in a microwaveproof bowl, cover and microwave for 6–8 minutes for 350g/12oz; and 7½–10 minutes for 450g/1lb, stirring and breaking apart twice. Leave to stand, covered, for 5 minutes before using.

SCAMPI

frozen cooked	450g/1lb	DEFROST	To defrost, place in a shallow microwaveproof dish and microwave for 7–8 minutes, stirring twice. Leave to stand, covered, for 5 minutes before using.

SMOKED HADDOCK

frozen fillets	175g/6oz boil-in-the-bag	HIGH	To defrost *and* cook, place bag on a plate and snip a couple of vent holes. Microwave for 5–6 minutes, turning over once. Leave to stand for 2–3 minutes before using.

SMOKED SALMON

frozen sliced	90–115g/3–4oz packet	DEFROST	To defrost, unwrap the salmon and separate the slices. Arrange evenly on a plate and microwave for 1½–2 minutes, turning once.

SOLE

frozen fillets	450g/1lb	DEFROST	To defrost, place in a microwaveproof dish with thicker portions to the outer edge. Cover and microwave for 7–8 minutes, rearranging once. Leave to stand for 5 minutes before using.

TROUT

frozen whole	2 x 225–275g/8–10oz 4 x 225–275g/8–10oz	DEFROST	To defrost, place in a shallow microwaveproof dish and microwave for 9–11 minutes for 2 whole fish; and 19–21 minutes for 4 whole fish, turning or rearranging twice. Leave to stand for 5 minutes before using.

WHITING

frozen fillets	450g/1lb	DEFROST	To defrost, place in a microwaveproof dish with thicker portions to the outer edge. Cover and microwave for 7–8 minutes, rearranging once. Leave to stand for 5 minutes before using.

Defrosting Poultry and Game

CHICKEN

frozen quarters	2 x 225g/8oz 4 x 225g/8oz	LOW	To defrost, remove any wrappings and place in a microwaveproof dish so that the meatiest parts are to the outer edge. Microwave for 7–9 minutes for 2 x 225g/8oz quarters; and 15 minutes for 4 x 225g/8oz quarters, turning over and rearranging once. Leave to stand for 10 minutes before using.
frozen drumsticks, about 115g/4oz each	2 4 6	LOW	To defrost, remove any wrappings and place in a shallow microwaveproof dish so that the meatiest parts are to the outer edge. Microwave for 4–5 minutes for 2; 7–8 minutes for 4; and 12 minutes for 6 drumsticks, turning over and rearranging once. Leave to stand for 10 minutes before using.
frozen thighs, about 115g/4oz each	4 8	LOW	To defrost, remove any wrappings and place in a shallow microwaveproof dish so that the meatiest parts are to the outer edge. Microwave for 8 minutes for 4 thighs; and 15 minutes for 8 thighs, turning over and rearranging once. Leave to stand for 10 minutes before using.
frozen wings	450g/1lb 900g/2lb	LOW	To defrost, remove any wrappings and place in a shallow microwaveproof dish. Microwave for 8 minutes for 450g/1lb; and 15 minutes for 900g/2lb wings, turning over and rearranging twice. Leave to stand for 10 minutes before using.
frozen boneless breasts	2 x 225g/8oz 4 x 225g/8oz	LOW	To defrost, remove any wrappings and place in a shallow microwaveproof dish. Microwave for 8 minutes for 2 x 225g/8oz breasts; and 15 minutes for 4 x 225g/8oz breasts, turning over and rearranging once. Leave to stand for 10 minutes before using.
frozen whole chicken	1kg/2¼lb 1.5kg/3–3½lb 1.75kg/4–4½lb	DEFROST	To defrost, remove wrappings and place, breast-side down, on a microwaveproof rack or upturned saucer in a shallow dish. Microwave for 12–14 minutes for a 1kg/2¼lb bird; 18–22 minutes for a 1.5kg/3–3½lb bird; and 24–30 minutes for a 1.75kg/4–4½lb bird, turning over halfway through the time and shielding legs, wing tips or hot spots with foil if necessary. Leave to stand for 15 minutes before using. Remove any giblets at the end of the defrosting time.
frozen chicken livers	225g/8oz carton	DEFROST	To defrost, remove from carton and place in a microwaveproof dish. Cover and microwave for 6–8 minutes, separating livers as they soften. Leave to stand, covered, for 5 minutes before using.

DUCK

frozen whole	2.25kg/5–5½lb per 450g/1lb	DEFROST	To defrost, shield the wing tips, tail end and legs with foil as necessary for half of the time. Place breast-side down in a shallow microwaveproof dish and microwave for 10 minutes; turn breast-side up and microwave for a further 15–20 minutes, rotating twice. Stand, covered, for 15 minutes before using. Alternatively, defrost for 5–6 minutes per 450g/1lb.
frozen duck portions	4 x 350–400g/ 12–14oz portions	HIGH then DEFROST	To defrost, place in a microwaveproof dish and microwave on HIGH for 7 minutes. Turn over, rearrange and microwave on DEFROST for 10–14 minutes. Leave to stand, covered, for 15 minutes before using.

GAME BIRDS

frozen grouse, guinea fowl, partridge, pheasant, pigeon, quail and woodcock	1 x 450g/1lb 2 x 450g/1lb 1 x 900g/2lb 4 x 450g/1lb	DEFROST	To defrost, place on a plate or in a shallow microwaveproof dish, breast-side down. Cover loosely and microwave for half the recommended times: 6–7 minutes for 450g/1lb bird; 12–14 minutes for 2 x 450g/1lb birds; 12–14 minutes for 900g/2lb bird; and 24–28 minutes for 4 x 450g/1lb birds, turning breast-side up after half the time and rearranging if more than 1 bird. Allow to stand, covered, for 5–10 minutes before using.

GIBLETS

frozen	1 bag from poultry bird	DEFROST	To defrost, place in a microwaveproof bowl, cover and microwave for 2–3 minutes. Use as required.

TURKEY

frozen whole	2.75kg/6lb 4kg/9lb 5.5kg/12lb 6.8kg/15lb	MEDIUM	To defrost, place the bird breast-side down in a shallow microwaveproof dish and microwave for a quarter of the time. Turn breast-side up and cook for a further quarter of the time. Shield wing tips and legs with small pieces of foil and turn turkey over, cook for the remaining time. Microwave for 21–33 minutes for a 2.75kg/6lb bird; 32–50 minutes for a 4kg/9lb bird; 42–66 minutes for a 5.5kg/12lb bird; and 53–83 minutes for a 6.8kg/15lb bird, checking for hot spots frequently. Leave to stand, covered, for 30–45 minutes, before using.
frozen drumsticks, about 350–400g/ 12–14oz each	2 4	LOW	To defrost, place in a microwaveproof dish with the meatiest parts to the outer edge. Microwave for 12–16 minutes for 2 drumsticks; and 24–26 minutes for 4 drumsticks, turning over and rearranging once. Leave to stand, covered, for 10 minutes before using.
frozen breasts, about 225g/8oz each	2 4	LOW	To defrost, place in a microwaveproof dish. Microwave for 5–7 minutes for 2 breasts; 10–12 minutes for 4 breasts, turning over and rearranging once. Leave to stand, covered, for 10 minutes before using.

Chicken and Fruit Salad.

Defrosting Meat

BACON

frozen rashers	225g/8oz vacuum pack	DEFROST	To defrost, place on a plate. Microwave for 2–3 minutes, turning over once.
frozen joint	450g/1lb 900g/2lb	DEFROST	To defrost, if in vacuum pack, then pierce and place on a plate. Microwave for 8 minutes for 450g/1lb joint; 15–17 minutes for 900g/2lb joint, turning over twice. Leave to stand, covered, for 20–30 minutes before using.

BEEF

frozen uncooked joint	per 450g/1lb joints on bone per 450g/1lb boneless joints	DEFROST	To defrost, place joint on a microwaveproof roasting rack or upturned saucer in a dish. Microwave for 5–6 minutes per 450g/1lb for joints on bone; and 10 minutes per 450g/1lb for boneless joints, turning over once. Leave to stand, covered, for 30–45 minutes before using.
frozen mince	225g/8oz 450g/1lb 900g/2lb	DEFROST	To defrost, place in a microwaveproof bowl and microwave for 5 minutes for 225g/8oz; 9–10 minutes for 450g/1lb; and 17–18 minutes for 900g/2lb, breaking up twice during the cooking time. Leave to stand for 5–10 minutes before using.
frozen stewing or braising steak cubes	225g/8oz 450g/1lb	DEFROST	To defrost, place in a shallow microwaveproof dish and microwave for 5–7 minutes for 225g/8oz; 8–10 minutes for 450g/1lb, stirring twice. Leave to stand 5–10 minutes before using.
frozen hamburgers	4 x 115g/4oz	DEFROST	To defrost, place on absorbent kitchen paper and microwave for 10–12 minutes, turning over and rearranging twice. Leave to stand 2–3 minutes before using.
frozen steaks	1 x 175–225g/6–8oz 4 x 115–175g/4–6oz 2 x 225g/8oz	DEFROST	Place on a plate. Cover and microwave for 4 minutes for 1 x 175–225g/6–8oz steak, 4–6 minutes for 4 x 115–175g/4–6oz steaks; and 6–8 minutes for 2 x 225g/8oz steaks; turning over once. Leave to stand, covered, for 5–10 minutes before using.

GAMMON

frozen uncooked joint	450g/1lb 900g/2lb	DEFROST	To defrost, place joint on a plate and microwave for 4–5 minutes for a 450g/1lb joint; and 8–10 minutes for a 900g/2lb joint. Leave to stand, covered, for 10–15 minutes before using.
frozen steaks	2 x 115g/4oz 4 x 115g/4oz	DEFROST	To defrost, place on a plate and microwave for 3–5 minutes for 2 x 115g/4oz steaks; and 7–9 minutes for 4 x 115g/4oz steaks, turning over once. Leave to stand for 5 minutes before using.

HAM

frozen uncooked joint	450g/1lb 900g/2lb	DEFROST	To defrost, place the joint on a plate and microwave for 4–5 minutes for a 450g/1lb joint; and 8–10 minutes for a 900g/2lb joint, turning over once. Leave to stand, covered, for 10–15 minutes before using.
frozen sliced cooked	115g/4oz packet	DEFROST	To defrost, place on a plate and microwave for 3–4 minutes, turning over once. Leave to stand for 5 minutes before using.

KIDNEYS

frozen lamb's, pig's or ox	2 lamb's 4 lamb's 2 pig's 4 pig's 225g/8oz ox 450g/1lb ox	DEFROST	To defrost, place in a microwaveproof bowl, cover and microwave for 1½–2 minutes for 2 lamb's; 4 minutes for 4 lamb's; 4 minutes for 2 pig's; 7–8 minutes for 4 pig's; 6 minutes for 225g/8oz ox; and 9–10 minutes for 450g/1lb ox kidney, rearranging 3 times. Leave to stand, covered, for 5 minutes before using.

LAMB

frozen chops	2 x 115–175g/4–6oz loin chops 4 x 115–175g/4–6oz loin chops 2 x 115–175g/4–6oz chump chops 4 x 115–175g/4–6oz chump chops	DEFROST	To defrost, place on a microwaveproof roasting rack and microwave for 3–4 minutes for 2 x 115–175g/4–6oz loin chops; 6–8 minutes for 4 x 115–175g/4–6oz loin chops; 3–4 minutes for 2 x 115–175g/4–6oz chump chops; and 6–8 minutes for 4 x 115–175g/4–6oz chump chops, turning over and rearranging once. Leave to stand, covered, for 10 minutes before using.
frozen uncooked joint	per 450g/1lb boned and rolled joint per 450g/1lb joints on bone	DEFROST	To defrost, place joint on a microwaveproof roasting rack or upturned saucer in a dish. Microwave both types of joint for 5–6 minutes per 450g/1lb, turning over once. Leave to stand, covered, for 30–45 minutes, before using.

LIVER

frozen slices	225g/8oz 450g/1lb	DEFROST	To defrost, spread slices on a plate. Cover and microwave for 4–5 minutes for 225g/8oz; and 8–9 minutes for 450g/1lb, turning twice. Leave to stand, covered, for 5 minutes before using.

PORK

frozen chops	2 x 115–175g/4–6oz loin 4 x 115–175g/4–6oz loin 2 x 225g/8oz chump 2 x 225g/8oz chump	DEFROST	To defrost, place on a microwaveproof roasting rack and microwave for 3–4 minutes for 2 x 115–175g/4–6oz loin chops; 6–8 minutes for 4 x 115–175g/4–6oz loin chops; 7–9 minutes for 2 x 225g/8oz chump chops; and 14–16 minutes for 4 x 225g/8oz chump chops, turning and rearranging once. Leave to stand for 10 minutes before using.
frozen fillet or tenderloin	350g/12oz per 450g/1lb	DEFROST	To defrost, place on a microwaveproof roasting rack and microwave for 3–4 minutes for a 350g/12oz fillet or tenderloin; and 5–6 minutes per 450g/1lb, turning over once. Leave to stand for 10 minutes before using.
frozen uncooked joint	per 450g/1lb joint on bone per 450g/1lb boneless joints	DEFROST	To defrost, place joint on a microwaveproof roasting rack or upturned saucer in a dish. Microwave both types of joint for 7–8 minutes per 450g/1lb, turning over once. Leave to stand, covered, for 20–45 minutes before using.

SAUSAGEMEAT

frozen	450g/1lb	DEFROST	To defrost, remove any wrappings and place in a shallow microwaveproof dish. Cover and microwave for 6–8 minutes, breaking up twice. Leave to stand, covered, for 4–5 minutes before using.

SAUSAGES

frozen	4 standard 8 standard 8 chipolatas 16 chipolatas	DEFROST	To defrost separated or linked sausages, place on a plate, cover and microwave for 3–4 minutes for 4 standard; 5–6 minutes for 8 standard; 3 minutes for 8 chipolatas; and 5 minutes for 16 chipolatas, separating, turning over and rearranging twice. Leave to stand, covered, for 2–5 minutes before using.

VEAL

frozen chops	2 4 6	DEFROST	To defrost, arrange in a microwaveproof dish so that the thicker portions are to the outer edge. Cover and microwave for 5–6 minutes for 2 chops; 8–10 minutes for 4 chops; and 12–15 minutes for 6 chops, turning and rearranging twice. Leave to stand, covered, for 5–10 minutes before using.
frozen roast	900g/2lb 1.5kg/3–3½lb 1.75kg/4–4½lb 2.25kg/5–5¼lb	DEFROST	To defrost, place in a microwaveproof dish and microwave for 16–18 minutes for a 900g/2lb joint; 24–27 minutes for a 1.5kg/3–3½lb joint; 32–36 minutes for a 1.75kg/4–4½lb joint; and 40–45 minutes for a 2.25kg/5–5¼lb joint, turning twice. Shield any thinner areas with foil as they defrost. Leave to stand, covered, for 10–20 minutes before using.

General Defrosting Chart

BISCUITS frozen	225g/8oz	DEFROST	Arrange in a circle around the edge of a plate. Microwave for 1–1½ minutes, turning over once halfway through cooking. Leave to stand for 5 minutes before serving.
BREAD frozen large white or brown sliced or uncut loaf	800g/1¾lb	DEFROST	Loosen wrapper but do not remove. Microwave for 4 minutes. Leave to stand for 5 minutes before slicing or removing ready-cut slices. Leave a further 10 minutes before serving.
frozen individual bread slices and rolls	1 slice/1 roll 2 slices/2 rolls 4 slices/4 rolls	DEFROST	Wrap loosely in kitchen paper and microwave for ¼–½ minute for 1 slice/1 roll; ½–1 minute for 2 slices/2 rolls; and 1½–2 minutes for 4 slices/4 rolls. Leave to stand for 2 minutes before serving.
frozen pitta bread	2 4	DEFROST	Place on a double thickness piece of kitchen paper and microwave for 1½–2 minutes for 2 pittas; and 2–3 minutes for 4 pittas, turning once halfway through the cooking time.
frozen crumpets	2 4	HIGH	To defrost *and* reheat. Place on a double thickness piece of kitchen paper and microwave for ½–¾ minute for 2 crumpets; 1–1½ minutes for 4 crumpets, turning once.
CAKES frozen small light fruit cake	small light fruit cake 1 slice	DEFROST	To defrost, place on a microwaveproof rack and microwave, uncovered, for 5 minutes for a whole small cake; ½–¾ minute for 1 slice, rotating twice. Leave to stand for 10 minutes before serving.
frozen Black Forest gâteau	15cm/6in gâteau	DEFROST	To defrost, place on a serving plate and microwave, uncovered, for 4–6 minutes, checking constantly. Leave to stand for 30 minutes before serving.
frozen cream sponge	15cm/6in sponge	HIGH	To defrost, place on a double thickness piece of kitchen paper and microwave for 45 seconds. Leave to stand for 10–15 minutes before serving.
frozen jam sponge	15–18cm/6–7in sponge	DEFROST	To defrost, place on a double thickness piece of kitchen paper and microwave for 3 minutes. Leave to stand for 5 minutes before serving.
frozen small sponge buns	2 4	DEFROST	To defrost, place on a rack and microwave for 1–1½ minutes for 2 buns; and 1½–2 minutes for 4 buns, checking frequently. Leave to stand for 5 minutes before serving.
frozen chocolate éclairs	2	DEFROST	To defrost, place on a double thickness sheet of kitchen paper and microwave for ¾–1 minute. Leave to stand 5–10 minutes before serving.
frozen doughnuts	2 x cream filled 2 x jam filled	DEFROST	To defrost, place on a double thickness sheet of kitchen paper and microwave for 1–1½ minutes for 2 cream-filled doughnuts; and 1½–2 minutes for 2 jam-filled doughnuts. Leave to stand 3–5 minutes before serving.
CASSEROLES frozen	2 servings 4 servings	HIGH	To defrost *and* reheat. Place in a microwaveproof dish, cover and microwave for 8–10 minutes for 2 servings; 14–16 minutes for 4 servings, breaking up and stirring twice as the casserole thaws. Leave to stand, covered, for 3–5 minutes before serving.
CHEESECAKE frozen	individual fruit-topped individual cream-topped family-size fruit-topped family-size cream-topped	DEFROST	To defrost, remove from container and place on a microwaveproof serving plate. Microwave for 1–1½ minutes for individual fruit-topped; 1–1¼ minutes for individual cream-topped; 5–6 minutes for family-size fruit-topped; and 1½–2 minutes for family-size cream-topped, rotating once and checking frequently. Leave to stand for 5–15 minutes before serving.

CREPES OR PANCAKES frozen	8	MEDIUM	To defrost, place a stack of 8 crêpes or pancakes on a plate and microwave for 1½–2 minutes, rotating once. Leave to stand for 5 minutes, then peel apart to use.
CROISSANTS frozen	2 4	DEFROST	To defrost, place on a double thickness piece of kitchen paper and microwave for ½–1 minute for 2 croissants; and 1½–2 minutes for 4 croissants.
FISH IN SAUCE frozen boil-in-the bag	1 x 170g/6oz 2 x 170g/6oz	DEFROST or MEDIUM	To defrost *and* cook, pierce the bag and place on a plate. Microwave for 11–12 minutes on DEFROST for 1 x 170g/6oz bag; and 10–12 minutes on MEDIUM for 2 x 170g/6oz bags. Shake gently to mix, leave to stand for 2 minutes then snip open to serve.
FLANS & QUICHES frozen unfilled cooked flans	15–18cm/6–7in	DEFROST	To defrost, place on a plate and microwave for 1–1½ minutes. Leave to stand for 5 minutes before using.
frozen filled cooked flans	10cm/4in 20cm/8in	HIGH	To defrost *and* cook, place on a plate and microwave for 1–1½ minutes for a 10cm/4in flan; and 2½–3½ minutes for a 20cm/8in flan. Leave to stand for 5 minutes before serving or using.
FRUIT CRUMBLE frozen cooked frozen uncooked	made with 900g/2lb prepared fruit and 175g/6oz crumble topping (to serve 4)	DEFROST *then* HIGH	To defrost *and* cook, microwave frozen cooked crumble for 15 minutes on DEFROST, then 5 minutes on HIGH; and frozen uncooked crumble for 15 minutes on DEFROST, then 10–14 minutes on HIGH, until cooked or reheated.
LASAGNE frozen prepared	450g/1lb	DEFROST *then* HIGH	To defrost *and* cook, remove any foil packaging and place in a microwave-proof dish. Cover and microwave on DEFROST for 8 minutes. Allow to stand for 5 minutes, then microwave on HIGH for 8–9 minutes. Brown under a preheated hot grill if liked.
ORANGE JUICE frozen concentrated	175ml/6fl oz carton	HIGH	To defrost, remove lid and place in a microwaveproof jug. Microwave for 1–1½ minutes, stirring once. Add water to dilute and serve.
PASTA frozen cooked	275g/10oz	DEFROST	To defrost *and* reheat, place in a microwaveproof dish, cover and microwave for 10 minutes, stirring twice. Leave to stand, covered, for 2–3 minutes before serving.
PASTRY frozen shortcrust and puff	200g/7oz packet 400g/14oz packet	DEFROST	Do not remove from wrappings unless unsuitable for microwave. Microwave for 2½–3 minutes for a 200g/7oz packet; and 4 minutes for a 400g/14oz packet. Leave to stand for 3 minutes before using.
PATE frozen	115g/4oz pack 200g/7oz pack 275g/10oz slice	DEFROST	Unwrap and place on a plate or leave in dish if suitable for microwave. Cover and microwave for 1 minute for 115g/4oz pack; 3–4 minutes for 200g/7oz pack; and 3–4 minutes for 275g/10oz slice, rotating 2–3 times. Leave to stand for 15–20 minutes before serving.
PIZZA frozen	30cm/12in 13cm/5in	HIGH	To defrost *and* cook. Place on a plate and microwave for 3–5 minutes for a 30cm/12in pizza; and 1½–2 minutes for a 13cm/5in pizza, rotating the dish twice.
RICE frozen cooked	225g/8oz 450g/1lb	HIGH	To defrost *and* reheat. Place in a microwaveproof dish, cover and microwave for 5–6 minutes for 225g/8oz; and 7–8 minutes for 450g/1lb, stirring twice. Leave to stand, covered, for 2 minutes before using.

SCONES

frozen	2	DEFROST	To defrost, place on a double thickness piece of kitchen paper.
	4		Microwave for 1¼–1½ minutes for 2 scones; 3 minutes for 4 scones, rearranging once.

SOUPS

frozen	300ml/½ pint/1¼ cups	HIGH	To defrost *and* reheat. Place in a bowl, cover and microwave for
	600ml/1 pint/2½ cups		4–4½ minutes for 300ml/½ pint/1¼ cups; and 7–7½ minutes for 600ml/ 1 pint/2½ cups, breaking up and stirring 2–3 times.

STOCKS

frozen	300ml/½ pint/1¼ cups	HIGH	Place in a jug or bowl, microwave uncovered: 2½–3 minutes for 300ml/
	600ml/1 pint/2½ cups		½ pint/1¼ cups; and 5–6 minutes for 600ml/1 pint/2½ cups, stirring and breaking up 2–3 times.

WHITE SAUCE

frozen and variations (such as cheese, parsley or mustard)	300ml/½ pint/1¼ cups	HIGH	To defrost *and* reheat. Place in a microwaveproof dish and microwave for 4–5 minutes, stirring twice. Whisk to serve.

YOGURT

frozen	150g/5oz carton	HIGH	To defrost, remove lid and microwave for 1 minute. Stir well and leave to stand for 1–2 minutes before serving.

Maple and Banana Teabread.

Index